SUSAN HOCHSTETLER

HOME LIFE
on the
PRAIRIE

OKLAHOMA

⊙ Oklahoma City

Clarita • • Coalgate

Red River

An Amish Family's Story of Life on the Oklahoma Prairie
with Community and School History

Home Life on the Prairie
Susan Hochstetler

10 digit ISBN 1-890050-84-9
13 digit ISBN 978-1-890050-84-9

© January 2005 Carlisle Press

First Printing 2005 5M
Second Printing 2007 5M

Cover art: Judy Kauffman
Text and Cover Design: Ann Troyer
Printing: Carlisle Printing, Sugarcreek, Ohio

Carlisle Press
WALNUT CREEK
2673 TR 421
Sugarcreek, OH 44681
1-800-852-4482

Contents

IV

Acknowledgments

WE WOULD LIKE TO TAKE THIS OPPORTUNITY to thank all of you who in any way provided us with information and material for this book—any photos, old letters, or diaries, and all the information given over the phone too.

We want to thank Norman and Sylvia Miller for providing us with most of the history on Oklahoma and Coal County, as well as material and information on the families who lived there. Also, we want to thank Ben and Esther Troyer for their information on the church records and families. May God bless you all.

We had tried to piece things together in story form, to the best of our knowledge. Some instances which we did not have dates for were used where we thought they fitted best. Not all happenings are down exactly in order as they happened. But all happenings are true and took place at one time or another on the farm in Oklahoma.

All honor and praise be given to God, our Heavenly Father. May we all meet on the Heavenly shore!

Martin and Susan Hochstetler

Introduction

H OME *LIFE ON THE PRAIRIE* IS FOURTH IN
a series of books written by Martin and Susan Hochstetler. Book 1—*Life on the Edge of the Wilderness*—is about
their life on the ranch in Horsefly, British Columbia, Canada. Book 2—*Farm Life in the Hills*—explains their life on
the farm in Holmes County, Ohio after moving back among
home folks again. In book 3—*Cabin Life on the Kootenai*—
we read about their experiences in the Rexford, Montana
area, on the West Kootenai.

In this book they have moved from Montana onto a farm
in the Clarita Amish settlement in Oklahoma.

Clarita, Oklahoma History

Here is a short history of Coal County, Oklahoma, long
before the Amish lived there. Oklahoma came from two
Choctaw words—Okla meaning "people" and homa meaning "red".

Before Oklahoma became a state in 1907, there were two
territories. Indian Territory on the east and Oklahoma Territory on the west. The five civilized tribes which made up
the Indian Territory were the Cherokee, Choctaw, Creek,
Chickasaw, and Seminole. They received their Oklahoma
lands from the federal government in the 1820s for "as long

The old Clarita post office was still in use when the Amish moved into the area.

as grass shall grow and rivers shall run" in return for their eastern lands.

Oklahoma Territory on the west was mostly reserved for the plains tribes.

Coal County was part of the Choctaw Nation, located in the southeastern part of the state with Coalgate the county seat. The first coal mines in Coalgate were opened in 1882, giving the town its name as well as the county. Mules were used a lot in the early days of coal mining. The first coal mined in Coalgate was done by shovel and scrapers and was near the surface. As long as the mines operated, the town flourished and was prosperous, being served by four railroads.

In 1897, Coalgate had a population of 1,500 and by 1900

The redbud is the Oklahoma state tree and this beauty is in Raymond Millers' orchard.

The old Clarita grocery store stands empty with windows boarded shut. Also a relic of bygone days.

it reached 2,600.

In 1921-22, the mines closed, due partly because the railroads started using more fuel oil and public utilities switched to natural gas or fuel oil. The use of the coal-fired steam engine dropped drastically. At the same time there had been three years of crop failures. The effects of the economy were devastating. Miners left the area, and farmers were unable to pay their loans. Banks failed and people moved away.

In the 1950s there was a brief resurgence of prosperity when coal was in demand again, only to last until 1958. Families had to look elsewhere for employment. Gradually many towns became ghost towns. A large amount of land returned to grasslands for stock production. Very little virgin prairie land remains.

The name Clarita was chosen in honor of the president

The new Clarita water tower stands big and tall beside the old one.

The new post office in Clarita today.

This is on the Martin Hereford Ranch where so many of the Amish men and boys worked for Gus Martin.

of the M O & G Railroad. A post office opened its doors in January 1910 and continues today. But most of the Amish were on Coalgate Route 5 mail route.

At one time the town of Clarita was a booming town with banks, hotels, restaurants, lumberyards, doctors, a drugstore, cotton gin, grain elevator, newspaper office, and blacksmith shop. Then came the Great Depression in the early 30s and many of these businesses closed.

When the Amish first shopped for land in Coal County, there was still a grocery store in Clarita, and one of the railroads was still operating. In 1982, the last grocery store closed its doors. The Amish then went to Coalgate for groceries and other business purposes.

Another step of decline for the town of Clarita was in the summer of 1988 when the last train running through Coal County stopped its run. Usually the chilling howl of coyotes indicated that a train would soon come through. Although the yipping of the coyote can still be heard, it is not so much all at one time.

Part I

chapter one

A New Home

THE COOL MORNING BREEZES COMING IN THE windows were very soothing as Susan dressed to go to the milk house and barn at 4:00 a.m. one morning in August 1985. The week before had been a scorcher. The 100 degree plus Oklahoma heat was hard to get used to. Then they had gotten three inches rain and it cooled off to eighty - ninety degrees with seventies at night.

As Susan walked to the barn she felt the cool breeze blow gently on her face. How thankful they had been for the rain and cooler weather.

The stars were shining bright and the Big Dipper was in the sky as usual. The North Star and the "W" were there too. This was always a comfort to Susan. God was still in control. For as long as she could remember, no matter where they lived, these stars or constellations always seemed to smile down on her in the evenings and early mornings—from Ohio to British Columbia, back to Ohio, then to Montana, and now Oklahoma. In the early morning hours God always seemed so close. His handiwork across the sky was so beautiful. *How could anyone ever doubt our almighty Creator?* she mused. Susan could not climb Olsen Hill as she had in Montana, to her special spot to have time alone with

God. But here under the vast prairie skies, under the millions of stars, she found that special spot.

As she swung the door open to the milk house to get the milker pails prerinsed and ready, Blacky the cat slipped in behind her with a friendly "meow". She was waiting for her breakfast of warm milk.

Just then the diesel motor started up and Susan could hear the cows coming into the holding pen. Mart had opened the outside gate. She quickly put feed in the six troughs for the first six cows that came in to be milked. Herbie the Border collie was in his place under the feed bin. He always watched to make sure the cows went into their stalls. When the first six were finished milking, he made sure they went out the right exit door. He loved his work but not all the cows liked him.

Susan opened the door to the holding pen and the first six cows came in. There was Beauty, Star, Daisy, Dixie, Pearl, and Rosie. About then fourteen-year-old Steven came into the milk barn to help with the milking, while twelve-year-old Edwin started feeding the calves and the horses. "Good morning," greeted Susan as she smiled to her sons. Then she remembered that not everyone was a morning person like she was. Not everyone wanted to smile and chat or sing at 4:00 in the morning! Getting up at that time in the morning was a rather rude awakening for anyone, especially school-age boys who never got up until 6:00 a.m. before. Their schedule was so different here in Oklahoma than it had been in Montana.

It was now time to change the cows. Mart let the cows out, Steven put feed in the troughs, and Susan rinsed and dipped the milkers. The next six cows to come in were Polly, Betsy, Molly, White, Spot, and Boss. There were three aisles. One person to each aisle. Each person did two cows. Wash, milk, dip, wash, milk, dip. It wasn't far to the tank to empty the milk buckets. Mart had made swinging doors at the end of each aisle and right on the other side was the milk house where the bulk tank was centered.

The third batch of cows were about ready to come in. The horses were ruffling in the horse barn. Edwin must be done with the calves and was feeding the horses. Here they come! The next cows were Blossom, Gentle, Twila, Tammy, Pansy, and Lilly. "Look out, Herbie!" Susan gasped. "You better be careful; Lilly doesn't like you, and she kicked to hit you, but missed." Herbie went back under the feed bin and lay down to lick his paws that were only nipped. That was a close call! Lilly was always rather jumpy. She didn't like Herbie.

Tammy was their highest producer. She milked an average of eighty pounds per day. Boss, Gentle and Twila were not far behind, averaging around seventy pounds per day.

Herbie was very much a part of Mart and Susan's farm life.

Most of the others milked from forty to sixty pounds. The August heat was hard on a dairy herd. That was one reason for milking so early. It was cooler, and the cows could graze after the milking before it got so warm. It was important to stay on the same schedule daily. So milking time was 4:00 in the afternoon too.

The last four cows to come in the milk barn were Ellen, Irene, Frances, and Jerse. There was one Jersey cow amongst all the Holsteins, to help put the butterfat up. There were two dry cows still in the holding pen. Gertie and Blackie were brought through last. Susan was usually done in the barn by 6:00 a.m. She then hurried to the shop which was also their home until they built a house. She had to pack three lunches and get breakfast by 6:30. It took a lot of baked goods to pack three lunches, for their growing boys and her hardworking husband.

The boys left for school by 7:00. They took Rocky, the standardbred horse, and the road cart. They had around eight miles to go to school one way. The schoolhouse (Lone Star) was at Melvin Hershbergers at the south end of the Amish community. Steven and Edwin stopped in Clarita to pick up their cousin Jeremy Miller who sometimes walked up to the post office to save them time. Every other day they would take Vernons' horse from Clarita on to give Rocky a rest. Sixteen miles each day is rather hard on one horse in this heat. Then there was the train track to cross too. Susan prayed every day that they wouldn't have to wait on a train. Every time she heard the train whistle she wondered if they were at the tracks. "Dear Lord, bring them home safely," was her prayer. School started classes on August 19th with Mary Hershberger (Melvins) as teacher.

Mart left for work at 8:00. He worked for a rancher by the name of Gus Martin five days a week since the field work was done at home. He was helping the rancher get his fall crops in, then he would start to work for Elmer Yoder's construction crew.

Mart had bought the harness shop inventory from Menno and Irene Yoder when they moved back to Ohio to the West Union community. Menno had also worked some for the same rancher Mart was now working for. Gus Martin raised registered Horned Hereford cattle.

During the day Susan would sew what she could on some of their orders for nylon halters. Mart didn't come home from work until 6:00 in the evening. By then the milking was usually done, so he worked in the harness shop after supper, making or repairing harnesses. They now had a busy routine family life with many adjustments.

Baking was a challenge for Susan since moving to Oklahoma. She baked four loaves of bread every other day since the bread didn't keep very long in the summer heat. And switching from a wood burning cookstove to a propane cookstove was quite a change. The bread wouldn't rise the same. It didn't look the same, and it sure didn't taste the same either! In Montana the bread always came out of the oven such a nice golden brown, and mouthwatering good. Now it was either almost burnt or doughy. But the women in the community could bake delicious bread and even sell it to the public! So with her sister Esta's advice and looking over some of the other women's recipes, Susan finally learned to bake good bread again. Coming from a high altitude to almost sea level really made a big difference.

In Montana Susan always kept a piece of bread crust with

the cookies in the cookie container to keep them soft. Here in Oklahoma cookies are never hard, but crackers always seem stale. And if she wanted her brown sugar to be soft, she just left her canister lid off for awhile. Another discovery was that the propane refrigerator they had did not keep food as well as their Montana spring water trough, that had water running through constantly in the basement.

The biggest adjustment for Susan was when her mother (Grandma Troyer) passed away in July. Dawdys had come to live with them in May. Now only three short months later she was gone, nevermore to return to this earth again. No more would they see her face nor hear her gentle voice. The tears flowed freely. She had written a note in her German Testament that read:

Don't weep for me when I am gone,
For I have only gone Home.
When angels beckon it's time to go,
Across the river I will row,
To take death gently by the hand,
And journey to the promised land.

Grandma Troyer had been diagnosed with cancer (lymphoma) four years prior, and after exploratory surgery and chemo therapy she would be in remission for awhile, but then it would come back again. She was very patient and never complained. She was very concerned that her children and grandchildren all serve the Lord. Her actual death came from a blood clot that went to her lungs. She was the first to be buried in the Clarita Amish cemetery. Following is a letter she wrote to Susan's sister Mary Ellen (Mrs. John B. Troyer) near Sugarcreek, Ohio. This was the very last letter she ever wrote.

Monday, July 15, 1985

Dear Mary Ellen and all,

Greetings in Jesus' name.

Will start a letter and see how far I get. Church is over here at Marts and I'm glad. Even if I couldn't do much of anything.

Edna's mom and dad are back (Ben & Alma Hostetler). She is so talkative just like Edna. They were here for church and supper both times, and last night they stayed for the singing too.

Susan just had to fix two dishes, the rest is brought in by the others. Last evening she made spaghetti and meatballs and a layered salad. The rest brought pie and pudding. The first time they had church she had a chicken with lima bean casserole and sloppy joe sandwiches. The rest brought cake and jello salad.

They didn't get everything done they had planned on, but we had church anyway. Now this morning the bulldozer went to work and in no time he had some trees and brush down, that you can now see the barn and beyond from here in the shop. The milking barn is done and they are milking fourteen cows with milkers now but are having all kinds of problems with the waterline. They got a bad batch of plastic pipe, and the water pressure is high enough to make them balloon and burst. So this morning first thing Susan went to call for new pipe replacement. Mart had to stay here with the dozer man.

I felt good enough that I could go over and wash the dishes and sort and pack church dishes.

Today a week ago I was to the doctor and he took two

gallons of fluid out again. I went to Esta & Vernons then and was there until Friday evening. Dad came too and painted Vernons' shop and barn. It was so hot there—100 degrees in the shade. They are at the bottom of a slope and lots of trees across the road where the wind usually comes from. The house just didn't cool off until about morning. They want to put up a few ventilators on the roof, to draw the hot air out. But Vernon has been so busy in the buggy shop, he hasn't come to it yet. I told Esta to get the ventilators now that dad is here, he can put them in. Her kitchen is small and the propane stove with all the pilot lights and the fridge just keep it warm.

It's much cooler here at Marts. They are up higher on a rise and there is almost always a breeze. It felt good to get out here again.

Well Elizabeth (Leroys) have another girl. Esta talked with her Tuesday morning but I just didn't have the strength to walk up there to the phone.

Tomorrow the post hole digger is coming. So they want to make a holding pen, and on Wednesday they want to get the rest of the cows. They'll be milking around twenty-four then. Some are dry.

This is after supper. Vernons are here. They brought the road cart up and Vernon wants to put new shoes on Dewy, their horse. They sold their mare, Judy, to the Texas man. He wants to use her in parades. He's had her a couple times and liked her.

It's clouded up again and no wind. Hope it rains and cools off. Today Steven and Edwin got a letter from Rexford, Montana, from Roman Schlabachs' boys.

They wrote it's hot and dry out there too. They had from 95° to 105° all last week. Lots of forest fires in that kind of weather. They also had loads of visitors. Susan said that's one thing she doesn't miss, as busy as they are now with milking, farming, and all.

Saw in *The Budget* that Vernon Troyers' Arvada is getting married. Are you invited to the wedding? What church does she go to?

I finally got that wall hanging done for Judy. The girls helped and I sent it to her for her birthday. She wrote us a 9-page letter in return.

Now a little breeze is coming up. My news seems to be all, so will stop for now. Yesterday forenoon while church was here, Herbie, their dog, went into the one and only flower bed and dug himself a nice big hole! The marigolds were just blooming nicely after the sheep clipped them off twice.

Dad (dawdy) writes Tuesday p.m.

Hello everyone,

Will try and finish mother's letter. As she was writing last night she felt sharp pains in her knee pit of the left leg. By the time I went to bed it was worse. Mother didn't sleep good. It got worse and all red down the leg. Susan thought maybe she got stung by something, but she would have felt the sting.

This morning I was almost sure it was a blood clot and I went to neighbors, Noah Coblentz's, and got some fresh comfrey leaves. I put two on and gave her Bufferin. By noon it was better and the redness was better too. She had fever last night and had to have a cover.

Susan went to call the doctor and he said he would

send a nurse out to check her. By noon or an hour later the nurse was here. Esta came too with Kitty. Then the nurse called the doctor and said, "It is a blood clot." Now Kitty took Esta to Coalgate to pick up prescriptions that the doctor called in.

Yes, church is over and you weren't here. But we didn't expect you to be. Wonder if it quit raining now so they could move the trailer out? Hope I can come in this fall and paint the barn yet. We never know what God has for us.

Esta is back so I'll sign off. Good luck and take care.

Dad

Machets Gute. Seid uns eingedenkt. Mir auch gesinnet in schwachheit.

Grandpa mailed the above letter but before Mary Ellen got it, Grandma Troyer had passed on. The squad had taken her and Grandpa to the Ada Hospital Wednesday morning. That same day God called her home. It all happened so fast. Susan was in a daze. She had gone with another driver. She and Grandpa were both there when she went into a coma, and about thirty minutes later she was gone. Vernon and Esta didn't make it to the hospital in time. Arrangements followed.

By the time Susan came home from the hospital the neighbor women were already there canning green beans and helping in any way they could. The men came to help Mart as this was the day the rest of their cows were coming. Susan had never realized before how thankful she was that they had the privilege to be born and raised in an Amish community where no matter where you live, the people just come and take over at a time like this and help get ready for the viewing and funeral. The brotherhood and brotherly love is so kind and helpful.

Grandpa Troyer had stayed for about a month after the funeral. Then he went to visit his daughters, Mary Ellen (Sugarcreek, Ohio) and Elizabeth (Topeka, Indiana) and their families. He got the flu soon after reaching Ohio. After he was well again he left for Sarasota, Florida, where he had a job doing lawn work and landscaping services. He and Grandma had spent most of their winters in Florida since 1965. Thus they were called "Florida Dawdys" by all their grandchildren.

Now Florida Mommy was gone and Florida Dawdy on his way back to Florida. And Susan had thought they could spend many happy days together yet. But God had other plans. The little red shanty which had served as Mart and Susan's living quarters the first months in Montana, and later a bath house, guest cabin, and tack shop had been re-painted and fixed up on the inside, and served as Florida Dawdys' living quarters. They had built a small platform between the shanty and the shop. Now it seemed so empty. God had called a loved one home. His will be done.

Steven and Edwin faced major adjustments in school. New books, a new teacher, new faces, but also new friends.

They were also introduced to the chiggers which were plentiful all around. They are tiny insects that dig under the skin. It swells up and itches. They seem to attack newcomers in earnest. Especially after cleaning out fencerows and help-ing their dad make new fence. But in time they adjusted and didn't even care when someone called them an Okie.

Susan also learned that if you open the mailbox and saw

a scorpion, you didn't scream, you picked up a stone or stick and killed it and went about your work. If she saw a big hairy tarantula on the shop floor that somehow found a crack to crawl in, she would quickly grab the flyswatter with the long handle and give it a big swat. Adjusting in a new climate and coming from the mountains to the prairie was now part of life. Susan decided she could make it easier or harder to adjust. The choice was hers.

chapter two

A Mysterious Thief

AFTER MART HAD LEFT FOR WORK AT 8:00, Susan hurriedly started the laundry. The washing machine was out under the big hackberry tree.

As she hung up the laundry she heard the scissor-tailed flycatcher singing. What a lovely bird with a streaming long tail! In flight this beautiful bird opens and shuts its tail like a pair of scissors. Its sides and wing linings are a soft salmon pink, with the wings being black and a touch of red at the shoulders. This all stands out on the pearly gray back and neck with a white breast. This is the Oklahoma state bird and such a joy to watch as it flies from fence post to fence post. Sometimes it flies straight up in the air, then dives down with its tail going like a pair of scissors. The male has a famous sky dance, (especially in the spring) which is quite noteworthy and graceful.

After the laundry was all on the line and flapping in the wind, Susan started sweeping the concrete floor of their makeshift home. All at once she heard a thump as plain as if it were in the next room, or even overhead in the loft. The shop, which would serve as their home for several years, had a loft over the kitchen and dining area. Their bed was squeezed in next to the north window, and the china hutch served as a divider between the bed and dining area.

Thump! There it was again. What could it be? Susan went to the east part of the shop where Mart sewed harnesses and there they had bolt and screw bins and harness hardware. There was just a heavy curtain between there and the dining area. The can shelves were along the inside wall. She looked all around, but saw nothing. All was quiet. She stood there for awhile, thinking any minute something might thump again. After awhile she gave up and went back to the dining area to finish sweeping the floor.

There it was again! A real loud thump this time. But every time she went to investigate, all fell silent. "There must be a critter in this shop!" she said loudly. "We've got to do something about this."

Finally Susan got her pen and tablet out to write a letter to Grandma Hochstetler. She had broken her hip and was laid up.

Just then a calf bawled loudly out in the calf pen. A terrified call. Susan ran out to the barnyard to see what was wrong. She couldn't see anything unusual. Maybe a coyote had run across the barnyard and frightened the calf. It was running around in circles. It was very obvious something had frightened it. Susan opened the door to the calf pen and swoosh, the calf darted past her and galloped out to the open field, bawling as it went. There was no yard fence up yet, so the cows grazed all over, right up to the shop.

The dairy herd was way down along the edge of the south field near the woods. The calf took off in that direction and seemed to pick up speed as it went. Now what? Susan had no choice but to go after it. She saw the calf getting closer and closer to the dairy herd. The herd started running towards the calf. But once it was there, the cows slowed down to a walk and nosed the calf around to their satisfaction, then started grazing. But the calf still had to be taken back to the barnyard or it might try to get some milk. The mother cow and some others would probably let it drink.

Susan started back towards the barn. She called the lead cow and sure enough it started coming and the whole herd followed, with the calf in the midst. It seemed to take a long time to get back to the barnyard. The cows were put in the holding pen, and the calf went right along in. Susan cornered the calf and put it through the milk barn and out the milk house to its pen. Susan had grabbed a couple twines to use as a rope and once the calf was back in its pen she double-checked to make sure the door was closed properly. She then let the cows out to pasture to graze again.

Upon entering the shop she had to think where she had left off. Oh yes, she was going to write a letter. But where was her favorite pen? She was sure she had laid it right beside the tablet when she'd left in haste. This was ridiculous! The past week so many things had disappeared. At night she'd hear something rattle in the kitchen. When she'd go to investigate, all was quiet and she'd see nothing. Spoons and knives disappeared. Pot holders were missing, paper clips were swallowed up, and pencils had a way of simply disappearing too.

Then one day she spied the hay grazer bag in the harness part of the shop leaning rather suspiciously to one side, although it was still tied securely at the top. Mart had one bag hay grazer seed left in the spring when planting, and had put it in the shop thinking it would be safe there. He thought it would be dry and free from critters.

Susan untied the bag and it was half empty. But how? She looked on the back side of the bag which had been against the wall, and there was a very small hole there where the critter had taken the seed out, probably one by one.

She then came to the conclusion that they had a pair of pack rats in the shop. But they must be different than Montana pack rats. You could smell those right away. And they were noisy and not sly as these.

The next thing Susan did was put closed packages of poison on the top shelves above all the canning jars. The feed man said this should kill any kind of rats.

The first night Susan lay awake for awhile but nothing happened. Mart was already sleeping soundly. He wasn't going to miss any sleep on account of a few rats. The second night she heard paper rattle just before dozing off to sleep. She was wide awake in an instant. Hopefully this would be the end of the pack rats. How wrong she was! He only packed the whole packages away in his cache without opening them. The third evening Mart put a big rat trap on the top shelves of the can shelves. That evening there was another thump from the loft down to the can shelves. The boys and Mart were sound asleep and never heard when the big rat trap went off. Susan smiled in the dark. Got him this time! But the flashlight beam revealed no rat, only a snapped trap. There was nothing to do but go back to bed and try to get some sleep. Four o'clock in the morning rolled around so soon. But try as she would, she couldn't sleep, knowing there was at least one and maybe two pack rats right above their bed in the loft.

Maybe if she prayed for their friends who were ill and for the church, the young folks, and the ministers she could forget the bothersome rats. The seriousness of life itself and faith in God was so much more important than two silly rats. She prayed that God would give her wisdom, patience, and guidance as they raised their two sons for the Lord. She asked for strength to be submissive to her husband and a good example in church to the younger women and girls. She often felt unqualified to be a minister's wife and asked Jesus to help her daily to do better. The clock struck twelve and soon after she dozed off to a peaceful slumber.

The next day sister Esta came to the farm with five-year-old Leona and two-year-old Steven who would soon have his third birthday.

They talked about the fall gardens. Susan wasn't sure whether she trusted the cows, the dog, and the sheep to stay out of their flower bed long enough to sow some lettuce and radishes. They decided to pull up the sorry-looking marigolds and sow the seeds right beside the shop. Then if it didn't rain they could easily water them.

They went through some of Mother's things and sorted clothes and put things in boxes. The shanty would be moved closer to the barn and used as a tack shop sometime in the future.

At 4:00 Susan went to the barn to get ready to milk the cows. The boys would soon be home from school and they always helped Susan with the evening milking. Leona and Steven played in the milk house with the cats. Esta was fixing supper and Vernon and Jeremy would come later. They would all have supper on the farm.

Mart came home just as Susan was washing the milker buckets and hosing down the milk barn. He said he would finish so she could go. She picked up Vernons' Steven on her way out of the milk house. She had seen the sheep buck close to the barn and sometimes he could be mean. Jeremy and Leona had gone with the boys to feed the horses.

Susan was about halfway to the shop when she thought she heard something. Just then Steven whispered, "Sheep buck comes." She told Steven to hang on tight and took a dash for the shop, but saw she wouldn't make it, so she turned around and yelled for Mart and braced herself for the blow, holding Steven tightly against her. Mart heard her shout and came running. The sheep buck respected him and ran out to the pasture where the ewes were grazing. One blow was enough for them both.

It had been a beautiful day and they all enjoyed their supper outside under the hackberry tree. The days were not so warm and the evening breeze felt good. Oklahoma had many nice sunsets, but not as breathtaking as the ones in Montana. So as the sun was sinking in the west Vernon and Esta and family left for their home in Clarita. Herbie the Border collie watched them go then lay by the front door where he slept each night.

Susan had almost forgotten about the pack rats until she heard the thump again that evening and again the next morning after Mart had left for work. She was now determined to find these pests one way or another. She crawled up the can shelves and pulled herself on the top board, then inched her way by pushing and pulling until she reached the loft full with all kinds of boxes. There were so many boxes piled high. Where would she begin to look? All these boxes could not be unpacked until they built a house.

Susan started going through box after box, but found no evidence of pack rats. Finally she saw a big box labeled

"Cherished items—do not unpack." She decided to try that one. It was taped shut, and it took awhile to undo all the tape and look inside. This was the box where all their gifts were packed from friends in Montana. Also Christmas gifts from family and special "Sunday best" items only used for special occasions. It would be nice to look at those things again. But to her dismay she couldn't see any of the five new wicker baskets that were supposed to be in the box. They were chewed up and lying in the bottom of the box and ruined beyond repair. What was this? Oh, her best tablecloth was in shreds! So this was the culprits' nest! And here were those pot holders that Simon's wife Esta had given her. The long-lost glove, pens, pencils, hairpins, spoons, knives, and oh, that beautiful painted calendar sister Elizabeth had given. This was too much! Susan was anything but calm. She felt so frustrated and at her wits' end as to what to do with the situation. Just then she remembered she hadn't even seen a hole in the box. Remembering the hay grazer bag she looked at the bottom. There at one corner was a hole chewed neatly in the box. But where was the critter?

Susan finally got off the loft and tried to concentrate on her work the rest of the day. That evening Mart told his distressed wife he would get a live trap somewhere. Ben J. Troyers visited one evening soon after and their boys, Bruce and James, said they would bring their live trap as soon as they could. Several days later the trap was set and that night the guilty were brought to justice. They were pack rats alright. A pair with no bushy tails and looked more like ordinary rats.

To Susan's great relief there were no more after this. She hoped she would never need to see another one. From then on, there were no more mysterious thefts.

chapter three

Autumn in Oklahoma

SEPTEMBER WAS COMING TO A CLOSE. THERE had been a few out-of-state visitors the past month. Mart and Susan were glad to see them stop in. They were more settled now, and the warm summer days were past.

The first week in September a load from Holmes County, Ohio stopped in. With the load were John Oren and Susan Miller from Charm, Mose and Anna Miller from Baltic, and two couples from the Sugarcreek area, Delbert and Anna Shetler and Jonas R. and Anna Yoder.

On September 17th Susan's brother, Ed Troyer, stopped by on his way to Texas to hunt. He very seldom came to visit, so this was a treat. He visited his mother's grave. He had an injured leg in July and wasn't able to be at the funeral.

The last week in September found Susan canning apple-sauce. She was using Jonathan apples. They liked the taste of these and they didn't need much sugar. She hurried as she was hoping to finish the hobbyhorse she was making for Vernons' Steven's third birthday. Then there was the cake to make too. Mart was trying to get the winter rye in on Saturdays. He also made two sets of harnesses on his two days off.

On October 4th the first flock of geese were seen flying

low. These were snow geese. Susan always marveled how God had given these wild geese and other migratory birds their instinct to know when and where they should migrate each year.

The snow geese migrated from Siberia, the Northwest Territories of Canada, Greenland, and from the icy shores of Hudson Bay, then south for more than 2,500 miles to Texas and the Gulf of Mexico.

Oklahoma was on their route to Texas and the Gulf Coast. Many snow geese would stop and feed in the fields. Some were flying high and never stopped in the Clarita area. The long V formations became a common sight. Sometimes Canada geese were flying with the snow geese.

The hummingbirds had all left by the second week in October. The newspaper had an article where the residents along the Texas Gulf Coast were encouraged to put out feeders and help "fuel up" the hummers before their trip across the Gulf to South America and the rain forest where they winter. There were always a few latecomers or stragglers who might have come from the north country.

It is awesome that a tiny bird can be so powerful and travel so far at such speed. A hummingbird can hover, fly straight up or down, backwards or sideways, and zoom forward so fast it appears like a streak and then it's gone. It needs a lot of sugar water and nectar from flowers to keep alive and going. The people in the Clarita Amish community were doing their share to help feed the tiny hummers during the spring and summer months.

One afternoon while Susan was folding laundry, Herbie the Border collie started barking excitedly. It was almost time to start getting ready for the 4:00 milking. Susan was

hoping the cows didn't get out through the fence somewhere. Upon investigating she found what looked like hundreds of barn swallows flying low in the fields. Or were there
thousands? She ran for the binoculars. She called for Edwin
and he came to watch too. Steven worked for Gus Martin on
the Hereford ranch on Saturdays and he and Mart weren't
home yet. Never in their life had they seen so many barn
swallows at one time. The neighbor's fields were covered,
the power lines were full, and the sky was dotted with the
sweeping swallows. The air was filled with their twittering. If
they came close you could hear their vit, vit, vit very plainly.
Sometime during the night they moved on. Early the next
morning they were gone. Not one swallow in sight.

On October 20th Ben B. Troyer from Stephenville, Texas
stopped in at the farm to see Mart. William L. Miller from
Dublin, Texas was with Ben.

Mart had purchased ten cows from Ben in the spring. Ben
and Emma had lived on the farm next to Mart and Susan,
across the road to the north. But they had moved to Texas
with their family to work on a dairy farm in November of
1983, about two years before.

Emma's mother, Anna Coblentz, and the elderly Bishop
Noah Coblentz were living in the smaller house on Ben B.'s
farm, while Elmer and Anna Mary Yoder and family lived
in the main farmhouse.

Ben had come to his farm on business and stopped in at
Marts to see how the cows were doing. He was kind enough
to let them make payments on the purchase of the cows
without charging interest.

Mart had also gotten some heifers from Ben which were

due to freshen in a couple months. Steven and Edwin named them Twinkle, Robin, Gloria, Misty, and Lady. Four more heifers joined the herd which Mart bought from Raymond Miller. These were named Kathy, Lula, Sparky, and Blossom. Their first cow named Blossom had been sold, as she was not producing enough. So the boys wanted another Blossom.

November brought a few frosty mornings, so the boys dug out their heavy coats and "zipple caps". The birds that sang so heartily all summer had flown south or ceased singing—all except the mockingbird. Susan woke up one night to the shrill call of the mimicking bird. It kept on and on and on. Finally she got out of bed and went to the door to see where the bird was. It was right outside on the big hackberry tree and would not stop its loud, shrill calls. Not even after Susan tried to shoo it away.

During the spring and summer months Steven and Edwin had kept track of how many different kinds of birds they saw since moving to Oklahoma. Their mother would add to the list too. By fall they had 63 species.

1. Purple Martin
2. House Sparrow
3. European Starling
4. Northern Bobwhite
5. Western Meadowlark
6. Northern Mockingbird
7. Northern Cardinal
8. Baltimore Oriole
9. Barn Swallow
10. Song Sparrow
11. Scissor-tailed Flycatcher
12. Great Blue Heron
13. Common Poor-will
14. American Robin
15. Brown-headed Cowbird
16. Killdeer
17. Great-tailed Grackle
18. Loggerhead Shrike
19. Brewer's Blackbird
20. Red-winged Blackbird
21. Mourning Dove
22. White-crowned Sparrow

23. Red-tailed Hawk
24. Cattle Egret
25. Ruby-throated Hummingbird
26. Yellow-headed Blackbird
27. Green Heron
28. Pileated Woodpecker
29. Northern Flicker
30. Red-headed Woodpecker
31. Brown Thrasher
32. Downy Woodpecker
33. Common Nighthawk
34. Eastern Bluebird
35. Carolina Chickadee
36. Great Horned Owl
37. Eastern Kingbird
38. Chimney Swift
39. Blue Jay
40. Bewick's Wren
41. Roadrunner
42. Olive-sided Flycatcher
43. Red-bellied Woodpecker
44. Turkey Vulture
45. Dickcissel
46. Common Grackle
47. Spotted Sandpiper
48. Wilson's Snipe
49. Western Kingbird
50. Brown Creeper
51. Yellow-billed Cuckoo
52. Dark-eyed Junco
53. Harris Sparrow
54. Chipping Sparrow
55. White Throated Sparrow
56. Sandpiper
57. Long-billed Dowitcher
58. Snow Goose
59. Canada Goose

Susan had been quite excited in the spring to find that the purple martins also come to Oklahoma to raise their young. She had really missed them in Montana. The rich, cheerful, gurgling calls and chirps were such a welcome sound to them when they moved to Oklahoma.

In Coal County the purple martins usually arrive March 1-8 and the last ones leave August 1-8. Susan heard that since purple martins eat only flying insects, they are, of necessity, a migrating bird. They migrate all the way to South America to the insect-rich tropics. The majority of them winter in the Amazon Basin, parts of Brazil, and north Bolivia. They are at their nesting colonies only four or five short months each spring and summer.

Thanksgiving was almost upon them. Before long the north winds would bring winter, snow, and ice, and the autumn leaves that had fallen would once more be covered for another season.

The Saturday before Thanksgiving Mart went with Susan to Mother's grave. It was the first and only grave in the Amish cemetery at this time. They wanted to trim and mow and clean up before winter set in. Susan was thinking of the song that is usually sung at the graveside as the pallbearers start shoveling the soil after the casket is lowered at burial. The pallbearers usually cover the grave while the bishop reads the first verse, then a group of men are appointed to sing each verse after it is read. The first, seventh, and last verses of the funeral hymn (11 verses in all) (*Lieder Sammlung*, page 189) go as follows:

1. Gute nacht, ihr meine lieben;
   Gute nacht, ihr herzensfreund;
   Gute nacht, die sich betrüben,
   Und aus lieb für mich jetzt weint;
   Scheid' ich gleichwohl von euch ab,
   Und ihr legt mein leib ins grab,
   Wird er wieder auferstehen,
   Und ich werd euch ewig sehen.

7. Seid getrost, ihr freund und brüder,
   Seid getrost, ihr schwestern gar,
   Seid getrost, herzliebe glieder,
   Gottes Wort bleibt ewig wahr,

Welches sagt: im Himmelreich
Werden die gerechten gleich
Wie die helle sonne leuchten;
O! dasz wirs nur bald erreichten.

11. Gute nacht, ihr meine Kinder,
Gute nacht, herzliebstes Weib;
Liebten wir uns doch nicht minder,
Als ein herz, geist, seel und leib;
Gott die liebe uns belohnt,
Weil in Liebe wir gewohnt;
Was in Jesu lieb sich kennet,
Wird auch nicht im tod getrennet.

1. Good night, my loved ones;
Good night, my bosom friends;
Good night, you who grieve,
And out of love now weep for me;
Even though I part from you,
And you lay my body in the grave,
It shall rise up again,
And I will see you eternally.

7. Be of good cheer, friends and brethren,
Be of good cheer, you sisters,
Be of good cheer, heart's beloved members,
God's Word remains true forever,
Which says, "In the kingdom of Heaven
The righteous shall shine
Just like the bright sun;"
Oh, that we might but quickly attain to it.

11. Good night, my children,
    Good night, my dear wife (or husband);
    We loved each other no less
    Than as one heart, spirit, soul, and body;
    God rewards us for love
    Because we lived in love;
    Those who are acquainted with Jesus' love
    Will also not be separated in death.

How fitting these words were. They were like a healing balm to Susan's grieving heart.

Life is so short. *Alle menschen müssen sterben.* (All man must die.) Let us prepare to meet our God.

The ride home on the spring wagon was chilly as the winds whipped across the prairie slopes. It was about milking time as they came home. The boys had started getting things ready in the milk house. With all four there to help each other it was done in record time.

Saturday supper was always easy to make as usually Susan made rivel soup. Mart's mother had told her how he liked his rivel soup when they were first married and living in British Columbia, Canada. It consisted of milk, eggs, and flour. Each one put salt and pepper on to their own taste. Since they were milking now, there was always plenty of milk. They could usually get eggs at the neighbors. Or if the banty hen wasn't setting, they could use those eggs if they could find the nest.

chapter four

Horsepower

ABOUT A MONTH AFTER MART AND SUSAN moved to Oklahoma, they bought four draft horses and three standardbred horses. The draft horses had belonged to Sammie Miller who lived in Rexford, Montana, but still had some draft horses in Milton, Iowa.

The two geldings made a fine team and were named Bob and Bruce. The two mares were named Cindy and Lindy. Cindy was sold to a man from New Mexico who needed a horse for his carriage business.

Rocky was an average buggy horse and not so big. The other two standardbreds were sold to new owners. One of them went to Texas.

Mose Gingerich had brought the horses to their Clarita farm. He also brought along the manure spreader Mart had bought from Sammie Miller.

Bob and Bruce looked so huge as they stood in their stalls in the barn. Steven had to stand on a five-gallon pail to harness the team that first summer. He helped with the field work until their school started in August. Mart had planted hay grazer in May and then wheat and rye for grazing and hay too. Steven was interested in working with the horses and enjoyed the field work. Edwin was more interested in helping with things in the harness shop.

Now George and Sunlight had lots of horse company. George was still used as a buggy horse and riding horse both. Both horses had come all the way from Montana to the prairies of Oklahoma.

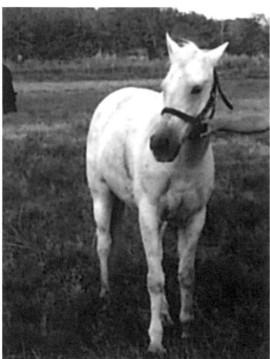

When Mart and Susan and the boys had first driven in the gate on their new farm, the first thing they saw was George and Sunlight in the cotton field. Quite a contrast from riding the cattle range in the mountains of Montana.

A local farmer had planted cotton on this farm, and the horses were put in the field as there was no barn

Sunlight in his younger years. He was in the pasture with a few of the other horses.

or barnyard or cross fences yet. Only the new shop building Mart had built with help from the community when he came to Oklahoma bringing a load of heifers and the two horses, before he brought his family. The heifers had been unloaded at Herman Yoders. They kept them and milked

This is Lindy and her filly which Susan named Lady. She was just that, an almost perfect filly. Very gentle and good horse manners.

them as they freshened until Mart had the dairy barn built.

Lindy was a pretty horse and Susan's favorite of the draft horses. She could keep up with Bob and Bruce when hitched beside them working in the fields. The horses were always allowed to rest at each end of the field. Herbie the Border collie trotted faithfully beside the horses as if it were his duty to do so.

Sunlight was often referred to as Sunny. He was a four-year-old part Arabian they had raised in Montana out of the grula mare that had three colts for them on the ranch. Susan still wished they could have brought Twilight, a half sister to Sunlight. Mart had let the boys pick which horse they wanted to bring along. Steven had picked Sunlight and Edwin had picked George. Mart had plans of taking Twilight too. But after the heifers were loaded and the horses put on, there was only room for two horses. So Mart led

Twilight back to the barn, and she never made it to Oklahoma. She was black with a white blaze and long legs. They had thought she'd probably be a good buggy horse. But they had Rocky now instead.

Mart helped Steven break Sunlight for the cart so they could use him to go to school to trade days off with Rocky. Steven was also trying to break a two-year-old gelding to ride for a local rancher.

It was now January of 1986 and Grandma Hochstetler had come to stay with Mart and Susan for about a month. This was a special treat for all of them. The January weather in Oklahoma was quite mild compared to the cold weather in Ohio. Some days it went up to the sixties and seventies. Then other times a norther blew in and the temperature could drop to freezing.

Grandma shared Susan's concern when using Sunny to go to school. She cautioned as the boys left, "Now please be careful at the train crossing." She was sure they felt they could handle the horse, and didn't always need her reminder. But they didn't know or understand a mother's heart.

Then one day as the boys came home from school, Susan was just ready to start the milking when she saw both boys jump off to try and hold Sunny. He was prancing around and took Steven around a couple circles until he couldn't hold him anymore. He crashed the cart against the corner of the barn and tore loose from the shafts. He then took off for the watering trough and jumped over it and broke off the board across the top. Now he was running outstretched across the south field, reins still dragging behind. Grandma watched with concern from the shop as Susan and the boys stood in disbelief as Sunny ran and jumped and kicked like a wild horse on down the field, farther and farther away, until he had most of the harness in pieces and off his back. The last they saw him he was headed for the woods at the far end of the farm. It was high time to start milking, so they had to get started and had to forget about Sunny for the time being.

When Mart came home and heard the story he said, "We'll just leave Sunny alone for awhile. Maybe he'll come home on his own. He would probably run away from us if we went after him now."

Susan never completely trusted Arabian horses. They were too spirited and high-strung for her. Sunny had always been their pet. But this had gone too far.

Sunlight never was hitched to the cart or buggy again. He was kept as a family pet and riding horse only and stayed with them for many years. He still lives with Mart and Susan and has become an old horse. He is just kept in the pasture during the summer and fed in the barn during the winter. His working days are over. He still nickers when Mart or Susan come to the barn. If horses could talk, he could probably tell them many stories.

One cloudy evening in late January, a tall Texan by the name of Bob Weed drove in at the farm to talk to Mart. He had bought a ranch close to the Hereford ranch where Mart worked, and needed someone to help him build a pole barn. This was how the Hochstetlers came to know the Weeds. Mart and the boys helped with the barn whenever they could.

Susan became friends with Bob's wife Delores who would sometimes come along to the farm and help with whatever Susan was doing. It was through Bob Weed that Mart later had some mares that were used on the farm and to help put up hay on the 260-acre lease down by the Boggy River. These mares, along with Bob, Bruce, and Lindy, provided a lot of horsepower to operate the farm. Mart also got a draft horse stallion at the Ada Horse and Mule Sale, whom they named Kansas. His registered name was Jim's Concord Farceur. But they didn't like any of those names, and everyone liked Kansas, so it was decided right off to change it for their own use but not on the papers.

Mart then made a heavy pipe and cable corral and runway for Kansas. He needed a runway for exercise because he was not turned out to pasture with the other horses. He was a very powerful horse, but not mean unless another stallion or gelding came close to his pen.

Good old George was not used in the buggy as much since Rocky came to live on the farm. But he was a safe all-around working or riding horse, good for many errands.

Three of the Weed mares grazing on the 250-acre lease in the spring when the grass was lush.

Bob Weed with Kansas and two of his granddaughters, Crystal (right) and Heather (left).

Visitors could take a ride on George, especially children, and no one had to be uneasy that he'd run away or buck.

George stayed on the farm as long as Mart and Susan lived there. The boys had outgrown the black pony-horse, so in the fall of 1991, before the Hochstetlers moved back East, George was sold to a Texan at the annual school sale.

Viscount Bunny, a standardbred stallion, also came to the farm to live in a new round corral. He was a gentle horse and Susan liked him. But she shied away from the Arabian stallion, Montey, which the boys broke to drive. She didn't feel at ease with this horse and her heart did several flips as she watched the boys in the cart, flying down the road, Montey's mane and tail floating in the wind.

Susan won't soon forget when Kansas got out of his runway and started fighting with Montey. There was quite a

Kansas in his runway which Mart built especially for him.

commotion until all was well again. Susan was helpless to do anything about it and had to go get Mart. Kansas was a powerful horse when he was fighting another stallion. It was the morning of the school auction and Mart had already left for the auction, leaving Susan to come later. Bob Weed's daughter Dianna happened to be at the farm and she took Susan to get Mart.

Although Susan never cared so much for Montey, she really did feel sorry for him because he was really beat up. He fought back and wouldn't have given up if it would have killed him. There was fire in his eyes and the will to fight.

Lindy finally did have a filly after several stallion colts. Susan named her Lady as she had such good, gentle manners.

Most of the horses were sold when the Hochstetlers

Viscount Bunny in his corral.

It's time for a break for both the mares and colts.

moved East again to West Union, Ohio in December of 1991. Sunlight and five of the colts that were born on the farm were kept and moved to Ohio.

chapter five

The Second Year

G RANDMA HOCHSTETLER HAD BEEN AT THE farm about a month when Mart's sister Ella and cousin Drusilla A. Miller came to Oklahoma to take her along home. They stayed several days to visit and see the community. They were amazed at the native Oklahomans (Okies) with their Okie accent and slow drawl.

While they were visiting at the farm Susan borrowed neighbor Elmer Yoder's buggy which had two seats facing each other in the back, and took Grandma Hochstetler and the girls to the south end of the community to visit Lone Star School where Steven and Edwin went to school. It was a very interesting visit. As they were leaving the school teacher Mary gave them each a little booklet which she had made, with the following information:

Page 1: *Little deeds of Kindness*
Little words of Love.
Help make the earth happy
More like the Heaven above.

Page 2:

A Favorite Recipe

11 boys   Mix well; season with plenty

5 girls	of books and material.
1 teacher (in good humor)	Garnish with visitors. Serve
8 parents (in good humor)	160 days a year with lots of
1 schoolhouse—cleaned	luck and loads of love.
regularly	

Page 3:

1985-86

Our School Parents

Herman Stutzmans	Andy Millers
Melvin Hershbergers	Dan Masts
Herman Yoders	Ben Troyers
Mart Hochstetlers	Vernon Millers

Page 4:

Grade 8:

Steven Hochstetler	May 21, 1971
Andrew Miller	May 28, 1972
James Troyer	June 19, 1972
Wilma Mast	July 5, 1972
Herman Joe Stutzman	September 20, 1972

Grade 7:

Lori Yoder	April 6, 1973
Edwin Hochstetler	April 16, 1973
Andy Hershberger	October 25, 1973

Page 5:

Grade 5:

Amos Miller	February 8, 1975

Grade 4:

Esther Hershberger	January 7, 1976
Tobias Yoder	July 10, 1976
Miriam Stutzman	July 15, 1976

Page 6:
Grade 3:

John Miller   December 29, 1977

Grade 2:

| Jeremy Miller | May 29, 1978 |
| Nathan Stutzman | August 23, 1978 |

Grade 1:

Sara Faye Yoder   September 16, 1979

Page 7:
Advice for Children
Learn while you're young
And not when you're old
For learning is better
Than silver or gold
Silver and gold
Will tarnish away
But a good education
Will never decay

Page 8:
Thanks for coming!
Best wishes from all of us at Lone Star School.

"What a nice gift," said Ella as they left the schoolhouse and stopped at Melvins' bulk food store. There were also some baked goods at the store. Susan got some flour and other supplies. Ella and Drusilla got some fresh baked goods which were enjoyed on the way home, with some left over for supper.

Grandma Hochstetler enjoyed this outing and said she really enjoyed her stay. It was such pleasant weather for the first week in February. Susan remarked that if this nice weather kept up she would soon be planting garden.

After Grandma and the girls left for Wayne County, Ohio, it seemed rather empty and quiet during the day. In the evening after supper Mart and the boys would work on the new fence to fence off the buildings, yard, and garden. This year they could plant a garden without trying to keep the animals out. Now they would have a real fence, and not just a temporary one.

Spring had sprung! The first purple martin scout arrived on the farm on March 4. Susan was thrilled to hear its cheerful gurgle.

Blackie the cat was seen climbing the pole to the martin box. She was quickly chased away. Before Mart got a predator guard around the pole she was seen perched on top of the box. "This will never do!" exclaimed Susan. Blackie the cat could no longer stay on the farm. Peppermint, an older cat, came to replace Blackie. She was a good mouser and caught mice in the hayloft.

The cows were feeling good now that spring had come. They were producing well with the new grass to graze in the pasture.

The heifers they had brought along from Montana were

second calf heifers now and had an average of 60.75 pounds
of milk per day. There were only eight left of the original
group. They were:

March 7, 1986

1. Polly	#11	54 pounds
2. Star	#30	58 pounds
3. Molly	#12	51 pounds
4. Beauty	#28	66 pounds
5. Pearl	#9	65 pounds
6. Daisy	#22	65 pounds
7. Dixie	#40	64 pounds
8. Spot	#21	63 pounds

Pearl belonged to Steven and Daisy to Edwin. It all started
in Montana when they bought a beef calf heifer with money
given as gifts (piggy bank money). At the time of the move
to Oklahoma both boys had a mama beef cow, a yearling
heifer, and a calf. They exchanged these for a Holstein heifer
with some money left over.

These Holstein heifers have quite a story to tell about their
young lives. In the fall of 1982, Mart and Susan and the boys
left their home in Montana to go visit Grandpa Hochstetlers
in Ohio. Grandpa was ill and was taking treatments. At the
time of their visit, he bought thirty-six calves from a dealer
near Farmerstown, to ship to Montana. Mart was to raise
them on the ranch for half. A Northwood Lumber semi
with Jeff Berky as driver (with a helper as second driver)
was to haul them out to Montana. The poor calves did not
know what all lay ahead of them.

Mart, with the help of others, closed up the semi with ply-
wood and put in fresh sawdust for bedding. The vet in Ohio
had to check them and give shots as they loaded them. He

gave a health permit and whatever they needed to cross into Montana. When all the calves were vaccinated and loaded, they put a canvas over the top and started to roll. Mart went with the semi, and Susan and the boys would travel back to Montana by train. They would hopefully meet each other in Whitefish, Montana.

The vet had given a permit to take the calves as far as the dipping station in Broadus, Montana, in the southeast corner of the state. Here they dipped the calves (which was required by law) in a large vat at a feedlot licensed to do this. It was freezing weather and the calves were pushed into the dip vats so they were immersed in the dip and had to swim twenty to twenty-five feet across to the other side to get out of there. After that rude awakening they were fed and left to drip about an hour, then loaded again to continue on their journey.

Steven and Edwin were all excited about the calves coming to the ranch. When they got to Whitefish, Montana and stepped off the train with their mother, there was no semi with bawling calves awaiting them. It had been decided if Mart is not there with the semi, they would get a room at the hotel until he came by. So after checking into their room and cleaning up, the boys were soon sound asleep. After waiting, watching, and praying and reading, four hours later, Susan heard familiar footsteps coming down the outside hall. Sure enough, it was Mart. Susan was very glad to see him and so were the boys, after being roused from their deep sleep.

They lost no time in running out to the semi where the rank smell of the dip filled the air, as well as the noise of bawling calves. Brrrr, it was a cold night and everyone (including the calves) was so glad when they got back home to the ranch.

The calves were unloaded at the barn and bedded with fresh straw. Everyone worked late to get the calves comfortable, watered, and fed before retiring for the rest of what was left of that night.

Mart made special pens in the barn for the calves and they spent the rest of that winter in the barn being grain fed along with good hay.

Come spring they were put on pasture in the basin where they grazed the alfalfa fields overlooking the mountains. They grew up to nice-looking young heifers.

The vet from Eureka came out to check them out by the end of the summer. Mart would keep his half and the rest would be sold to the vet if they passed the test for his program.

Several of the heifers Mart and Susan kept for their half tested out to be freemartins (females born twin to a bull calf). About nine times out of ten such heifers are sterile and nothing can be done about it. These had to be sold for beef. They would never have any calves nor give any milk.

The Montana heifers were growing into mama cows when moving time came in the spring of 1985. Six of the heifers had already calved before the day came to move them to Oklahoma. Mart was taking some of the machinery on this load with the heifers. Also some lumber to build a new shop on their new farm in Oklahoma. He built a pen of sorts that went in front on top of the machinery where the baby calves would go in. In the center of the cattle truck, the heifers went in next. There was a gate dividing the heifers and the horses which were brought on last. It was quite a procedure to load this semi which belonged and was driven by a local rancher. So amongst farm machinery, lumber, horses, and baby calves, these heifers once more started off on a long journey.

They had just left the Kootenai behind and crossed the Koocanusa Bridge when they stopped to check on the animals. Either the horses or the heifers had broken down the gate and George, the black pony horse, was flat on his side, with one leg sticking out of the back of the truck. So the gate was tied to the side and George was helped up on all fours with some wide-eyed heifers looking on.

After awhile they stopped again to check on things and one of the heifers was down this time, flat on its side, and good ole George was standing on its rib cage with his two front feet. Some circus this was! Mart got the heifer up and tied the horses in front near the machinery.

This was just the beginning of the trip. Many times they stopped to help one or more of the heifers up that was down on its side, feet sticking straight out with a frightened look in its eyes.

When they got to Missoula, Montana, they unloaded the heifers at the sale barn in a big corral. The little calves got their supper while their mamas were munching theirs. Mart finished milking the heifers after the calves had their share. While he was sitting there milking, a big airplane had taken off at the airport and flew right over the sale barn where Mart was milking. Every heifer looked up and watched that jet go, nose to the sky until it was out of sight. Mart never saw anything like it before nor since.

Several days later, after numerous stops to check on the heifers and to help the ones that were down on their sides, plus several breakdowns on the semi, they finally pulled into another sale barn late one evening in Stratton, Colorado. Mart had called ahead to tell them they were coming. Later, about ten or eleven o'clock, while Mart was milking the heifers out by hand, a sheriff car drove up. Mart thought now he'd have some questions to answer. Then a man came up to the fence and said in Pennsylvania Dutch, "Bisht du bissy? Mae nama iss Yedder. Ich bin von Kansas." (Are you busy? My name is Yoder. I come from Kansas.) Mart could not believe his ears! Here was a man who was now the town's mayor here in Stratton, Colorado, and he used to be a little Amish boy from Kansas. He was at the coffee shop along with the sheriff when a man from town came in and said, "There's an Amish man out by the sale barn milking cows, and that's no joke!" So the mayor and the sheriff drove out to take a look. This scene brought back many childhood memories of when the mayor helped milk cows himself in bygone days. It turned out he was a cousin to Andy Yoder from Rexford. Small world. Did the heifers think so too? They were probably just thankful and content to be on solid ground for one night and blinked their eyes and resumed to chew their cud contentedly.

After a long weary journey the heifers finally did reach Oklahoma. They were unloaded at Herman Yoders' farm where they were taken care of until Mart had moved his family down and built a milk barn. This was a strange land with wind and rain like these heifers had never seen before. But there were also beautiful sunny days and finally they too adjusted to the land and weather in Oklahoma. And they now graze with the other cows on Mart and Susan's farm, contentedly chewing their cud and swishing their tails to keep the flies off their back—those long, weary journeys long forgotten.

Yes, spring was now here, and spring on a farm means many new babies. There were new baby calves and little lambs. But the lambs would soon have to go as there wasn't enough room for sheep since the new calves were born, and Susan was ready to get rid of the old sheep buck anyway. Spring was a good time to sell lambs, so to market they went.

Then there were two little goslings. A neighbor had given the boys two goose eggs. The banty hen was incubating her eggs on a neat little nest in a five-gallon pail. When her eggs hatched, the boys took the chicks into the shop for Susan to care for, and put the two goose eggs under the banty hen to set for another twenty-four days, only to find she had hatched a pair of ugly ducklings. She turned those eggs faithfully, and they were about half as big as she was! What a dedicated mother! The boys brought the goslings into the shop for their mother to keep them dry. She wrapped them in a towel and put them in the oven on pilot. That was enough heat to dry them off and get them a honking and squirming around. Then Susan put food and water in a box with the goslings.

By this time the chicks were over three weeks old and wouldn't accept their mother, and she didn't want them either. So both goslings and chicks were motherless. They fared quite well by themselves when penned up at night so the night predators couldn't get them. They became family pets.

Susan had looked forward to the new foal on the farm. But Lindy's colt was born dead. So there was no foal to frolic in the fields this spring. Maybe next spring.

Peppermint the cat left the hayloft one evening when the spring peepers were singing merrily. She made her way slowly to the shop where the mistress and her family lived. The moon was bright and most of the other farm animals had bedded down for the night. There was still a light shining out through the shop window, so Peppermint knew what she wanted to do. She hopped on the platform that connected the red shanty to the shop and perched herself right beside the back door of the shop. About that time the night was filled with the challenging bellow of the Holstein bull coming down the fencerow, pawing the ground. The back door opened and the mistress stepped out on the platform with a big flashlight, shining in the direction of the bellowing bull, which was coming closer to the shop, but couldn't reach the shop because of the new fence that was now finished. Peppermint had the chance she was waiting for. She slipped in the door unseen as her mistress came out. She hid in a dark corner out of sight in the harness shop part. She found a place behind the long curtain in front of the can shelves. She heard the mistress come back in, close the door, and after awhile the light was turned off, and all was dark. Peppermint lay very still, not even purring.

During the night there was a chorus of meows in the bedroom. Susan hadn't found out that Peppermint had snuck in the evening before. The mother cat lay there as if she had all the right in the world to be there. Proud mama she was with four little kittens!

Mart went to fetch a box and put some soft rags in the bottom. Then he scooped up the cat and her kittens and put them in the box. He put the box by the back door so they could take it out to the hayloft first thing in the morning. Then they both tried to get some more much-needed sleep before the alarm went off at quarter til four.

Susan put the flashlight under her pillow and was hoping she wouldn't need it for the rest of the night. But sometime later she was aroused from her sleep again. This time she grabbed the flashlight just in time to see Peppermint coming with a kitten in her mouth, heading straight for the bed. There were already three kittens on the bed. Just then the alarm went off. Susan got dressed quickly and put the kittens and their mama back in the box and took them out to the hayloft. "Please, Peppermint, you are a barn cat, not a house cat, so keep your kittens out here in the barn where they belong!" Susan made a little tunnel by arranging several bales of hay. Hopefully the cat would feel more secure and hide inside the tunnel in the box prepared for her kittens.

Susan quickly climbed down from the hayloft to take her place in the milk barn. Another new day had begun. But she had no time to spend looking at the stars this morning as it was still cloudy, plus she had her hands full keeping the cat in the box on the way to the barn. Later tonight she could meditate and pray after the stars were out if it cleared off.

After the milking was done she took Peppermint some warm milk and to her relief she was still in the box in her hayloft tunnel.

April was such a lovely time of year in Oklahoma. The gardens were already growing nicely. The irises were blooming, as were the Indian paintbrushes along the roadsides. School was now closing its doors for another term. Wedding bells were ringing for teacher Mary. She was published to be married to Allen Yoder (Nelsons) on April 17. Allen was from the Chouteau area. This time of year seemed so fitting for a wedding, when everything was coming alive again after a winter's rest. Even the roses were starting to bloom already.

Mary had asked Susan to make the wedding cake, so she needed to practice with the recipe Mary had given. The cake needed to be just right. In a year's time, Susan had learned to bake cakes and breads in Oklahoma that were rising and baking the way they should, and yes, even fit to eat again.

Everyone was looking forward to the wedding day. Weddings didn't happen that often in the Clarita settlement. This was only the second wedding in the community. The first wedding had been on September 29, 1983, when Lena Mast (Dans) and Leroy Yoder (Elmers) were married. Allen and Mary moved to the former Menno Yoder place after the wedding.

The two days following teacher Mary's wedding Steven planted twenty-five acres hay grazer, on the eighteenth and nineteenth of April. Mart was still working part-time for rancher Gus Martin. Susan was hanging out the laundry on the day after the wedding, and was watching Steven as he made his rounds with the team in the hay grazer field, Herbie faithfully following at the horses' side.

All at once Herbie stopped and pricked up his ears and took off like a flash. Susan watched and wondered what he was doing. All at once she saw a jackrabbit running down the field in high gear, Herbie outstretched to his limit, trying his best to catch up with long-legged, big-eared jackrabbit. What a chase! Herbie didn't give up easily, but the jackrabbit didn't either. So around they went in big wide circles, into the woods and back out into the field until finally Herbie had to give up. He flopped down by the pond, his tongue hanging out, to rest awhile before taking a drink in the pond. After another rest he joined Steven and the horses again.

The hay grazer field had been worked up by an English farmer earlier. The Amish in the Clarita settlement sometimes needed to hire someone to work up the ground in spring or in fall depending on the weather, so they could get the crops in on time. (At the time of this writing the Clarita Amish church has now allowed tractor farming.)

After school was out, Edwin helped in the harness shop or sometimes helped Bob Weed on his ranch. Both boys had helped him off and on whenever he needed them to help with his new barn. The Weeds lived on their ranch only part-time. They still had a home in Corpus Christi, Texas at the time.

The last week in April, Susan was busy cleaning for church. Herman Stutzman's wife Dorothy came to help on April 30. It had rained for four days and now had cleared off to beautiful blue skies. A perfect spring day. The rains came just after the hay grazer was all in and Steven was done cultipacking. How thankful they were for the rain. God had provided again. The garden was doing so well.

The purple martins were singing so cheerfully. Susan went happily about her work. She and Dorothy cleaned the red shanty. It wouldn't be moved to the barn area until after church. She had washed curtains and couch covers and bedding. It was all flapping in the warm breeze. This was Wednesday. Mart had gone to help Gus Martin again. The boys were painting the milk house on this beautiful day.

That evening as the stars came out one by one, Susan stood out by the garden observing the constellations and handiwork of God. Mart was on the platform under the hackberry tree reading the Scripture text for church on Sunday. This was the time of year for council meeting and communion. How thankful they were to be able to partake of communion again. To hear again the story of the patriarchs and the beginning of creation. The Passover lambs as an illustration of the redemption through Jesus and His blood. *Yes, Christ Jesus died on the cross for our sins,* Susan mused. *Can I fully grasp the great love God had for me? Jesus' suffering and crucifixion. Can I imagine what He went through? The pain and the agony on the cross. Can we feel His great love for us, or do we reject it? He arose from the dead to set us free from sin. Do we let Jesus into our hearts when He knocks or do we turn away from Him? Jesus was a perfect example for us. What kind of an example are we for our children?* Susan thought about all these things and many more out under the stars and the big prairie sky. She prayed that Jesus would help her be a better wife and mother, a better example in church for the younger women and girls. Without His help she could not do it.

All at once something came loping up to the garden, nose to the ground. Quick as a flash, Herbie bounded upon it with several vicious woof, woofs. It was too dark to see very plainly, but Susan was sure the intruder was an armadillo. These came out mostly at night, and could root up the garden or lawn like a pig can. They had a real hard shell, so Herbie grabbed for the head. The armadillo got away, but Herbie kept it from rooting up the garden. "Good dog, Herbie." Susan patted his head. "You keep those things away from our garden."

An armadillo has nine bands or strips on its shell that slide upon one another. This shell is made up of many small plates of bony matter fitted closely together. One has to see it to actually realize or grasp how it actually looks or works. All these little joints can bend and allow the armadillo to curl up in a ball and draw in its head and feet. They have sharp claws and sometimes when in danger they will dig themselves right into the ground. The dirt flies high and fast. You want to keep your distance then!

The boys were coming home from the neighbors just then and Mart had finished his study hour, so they all gathered in the kitchen to have a snack before their evening prayer and Bible reading.

The main conversation was centered on the new teacher, Edward Yoder, who was coming to live in the community from Bloomfield, Iowa to teach the next term of school. The school would be moved up to Herman Stutzmans in the old house across the creek. Steven was now out of school and Edwin would be going by himself. It will be nice to only go half as far.

Florida Dawdy was coming back to spend part of the summer in Oklahoma. He had surgery in Florida, but was doing well. He would travel by bus.

Canning time soon arrived and the can shelves were filling up. Susan's mouth was watering for their first meal of sweet corn. But just before they could pick the first ears of corn, a bad storm flattened the garden. The night of the storm Susan dreamed she was out on the road when a big freight train came down the tracks, roaring and scaring Rocky, their horse, and they went for a wild spin. The roaring of the train didn't cease, and finally Susan woke with a start, realizing there was a real bad storm raging and it actually sounded like a freight train. A tornado! Was it really a tornado? But where could they go? They had no basement, and no cave to go to. Would they all perish? Hail was pounding on the metal roof of the shop building. All at once the roaring subsided. The storm had passed. How thankful they all were!

The next day they heard that a tornado had touched down farther south of the community. The hail and heavy winds had done extensive damage to gardens and crops as well. But the corn ripened on the ground, what wasn't broken off, and the tomato plants started new growth where they had broken off. So they had some tomatoes later on. Susan had already canned a lot of juice.

The purple martins were feeding their young and some had already fledged by July. In another month they would already be leaving to gather in great pre-migratory roosts. Their stay seemed so short.

One sunny Sunday forenoon in mid-July Mart and Susan and the boys were at Vernon and Esta's for brunch. Edwin had spent the night with teacher Edward who had come to the farm the evening before so Mart could shoe his horse. He had stayed for supper and Edwin then went home with him for the night and came to Vernons from there.

Grandpa Troyer was at Vernons too. He was staying there part-time and on the farm at Mart and Susan's part-time too. He wanted to go to Excelsior Springs, Missouri, to the clinic there for treatments, and Susan would be going along up when he went, to stay several days. They enjoyed a day together as a family again, but oh, how empty it was without Grandma Troyer. But life goes on. Precious memories are so dear.

Monday morning, July 15, brought the vet to the farm. Daisy was sick. The vet diagnosed it as a disease carried by the big horsefly. Now all the other cows had to have shots.

Steven was working in the fields again, sowing wheat and rye for fall grazing. He was hoping to finish with that today. Edwin helped his mother with the milking so Steven could go on sowing. But as the sun set in the west, he was still not finished, so he quit and planned to finish the next day.

That evening at the supper table Edwin was telling the others how the banty hen had hatched seven chicks and this time she was proudly clucking and scratching around to feed her new family when the goose appeared on the scene. The one gosling had grown to full size by now, but its mate had not fared so well. He had disappeared one night when Mart and Susan came home late from the Sunday evening hymn singing and forgot to pen them up. They had slept by the pond during the night and by morning the gander was gone. Probably a coyote had carried him away.

Edwin was describing how the goose had come up and tried to claim the little chicks and chase the banty hen away. Of course, she went into a rage and planned to tar and feather the goose. She fought for the life of her chicks and would have lost out had Edwin not come on the scene. He showed the goose who was boss and penned her up so the banty hen could raise her family in peace.

Poor goosey was lonely since her mate was not there. Maybe they could get a couple more geese or ducks so she wouldn't be so lonely.

Susan wouldn't soon forget how they had lost their goose

the year Edwin was one year old on the farm in Ohio. The gander was lonely too and watched over Edwin out in the yard. He claimed Edwin as his and wouldn't let Susan near without giving her a fight and black and blue legs.

The next day Steven finished sowing the wheat and rye, and started to cultipack. Mart was working for Yoder Construction. They were building a chicken house for Mayhart.

Susan had a large laundry flapping in the breeze. She wanted to bake extra bread, cake, and cookies to last while she was gone with Grandpa Troyer to Missouri. She planned a picnic for Mart's forty-sixth birthday which would be on the twenty-seventh of July, while she was gone. She baked a cake and fixed several dishes to take and sandwiches. They would be going back to the Boggy River one evening. Vernon and Esta and children and Grandpa Troyer would be going too. Lonnie Miller was in the area. He was from Michigan but at one time lived here. His wife Polly died early in the spring the year before. He then moved away and had now come back to visit. Susan invited him to come along on the picnic too. He would be good company for Grandpa Troyer. On the evening of July 23, they all left for the picnic. Once they got there the boys liked to swing on a wild grapevine, then jump into the river and swim out. Susan wasn't so sure she enjoyed that as it looked quite dangerous to her. But Mart thought it was safe. The picnic was a break from their hard work and busy schedule. The evening hours passed all too soon. The poor-will started calling. It was time to go home. As they arrived back at the farm, Herbie came bounding up. He had just chased another armadillo out of the yard. Good watchdog. It looked like he put up quite a fight this time as there was blood on his nose and ears. "Better be careful, Herbie," Susan cautioned. "Those armadillos can cut you open clear to the bone. Their claws are very long and razor sharp." Herbie wagged his tail as if he understood.

August 24 brought some visitors to church. Among the visitors were Minister Floyd and Betty Schrock and sons. They were overnight guests on the farm and their visit was enjoyed and appreciated very much.

It was time to think of planting the fall garden. Susan got her seed packets out that were left over from spring. She planted peas, green beans, lettuce, radishes, and turnips. Steven helped prepare the soil and make the rows. They sang as they worked. Susan knew their son was glad to be out of school and enjoyed farm and field work.

Edwin had just started back to school at Elm Creek. This would be his last year.

On August 26, Florida Dawdy left again for Indiana and Ohio, visiting family there. Then on to Florida where he stayed for the winter months.

From September 2 to September 19, it rained and rained, totaling nine inches. Everyone on the farm got the flu and chest colds. But the milking still had to be done twice a day, and the rest of the animals fed.

Peppermint's kittens were growing fast and could be seen playing in the hayloft. The banty chicks were feeding on their own and keeping the goose company.

More baby calves were added to the farm that fall. On September 29, Irene had a healthy heifer calf. It was always a plus to find a baby calf and a heifer at that. They were all quite happy about this.

October found Susan preparing for church services again. Saturday, October 4, before church the first time, the first flock of geese was seen flying low and feeding in the fields. The boys had spent the day at the Ada Horse and Mule Sale.

On Sunday morning when Susan came to the barn Mart told her Robin, cow #635, had calved. She had a healthy bull calf. Not all of them could be heifers, so they sold the bull calves for cheap prices.

On October 9, Melvin Hershbergers' son Abe married Lydia Yoder of Chouteau, Oklahoma. She was the daughter of Nelson Yoders. The wedding was in Chouteau. Mart and Susan and the boys were happy to be invited and were able to attend. It was a joyous occasion.

Mart and Susan were looking forward to visitors that were planning on coming the last week in October. They had church the second time on October 19. Communion would not be until November. On the evening of the 18, Blossom came forth with a dandy heifer calf. The boys and Susan did the milking so Mart could do some last-minute preparations for church the next day. Susan had gathered enough lettuce from the fall garden to use for church lunch with cheese sandwiches. Sometimes she made egg salad or if it was summer they had tomatoes. When it was cooler in the fall and winter they had hot wiener sandwiches. They would put them in the oven while church was in session. Then by noon they were ready. After church services were over everyone pitched in and helped get the tables set and soon lunch was ready.

Being prepared for church on Sundays was more than just having a clean house or shop and having the food ready.

To study the Scripture text and go over the songs that pertained to the Scriptures which often had deep lessons too, was just as important or more important than getting the place ready for services. The Ausbund (church hymnal) had many very touching lessons written by our Anabaptist forefathers that were good to study and take to heart. One must never take for granted the privilege we have of worshiping our Lord where and when we please.

Susan always enjoyed the hymn singings. She gladly make supper for the young folks and always some married people were invited back too. Whoever had church in the morning had the hymn singing in the evening. So after having church twice and the supper and singing four times, the bench wagon moved on to the next place.

On October 26 the visitors arrived at Mart and Susan's place. Monroe and Elizabeth Weaver, Susan's aunt, and Robert C. Schlabachs (cousin Ada) arrived with Jacob M. Miller as driver. Roberts' four sons were along, David, James, and the twins, Matthew and Mark. Also Roberts' oldest daughter, Betty Ann, and husband, Allen E. Miller, and their two little children, Emily and Steven.

Mart and Susan enjoyed their visit. It seemed like a long time since they had seen each other. The women marveled at the fall garden and everyone enjoyed the supper and singing. They had gone to see Mother's grave and saw a coyote on the prairie. They thought the prairie was a lonely place, but enjoyed it all the same. They did manage to see an armadillo when taking a walk during the day, just down the road from the farm.

All too soon their visit was over and it was time to go home. Susan made homemade biscuits with sausage gravy for breakfast before they left on their homeward journey. They visited at Vernon and Esta's place too.

The day the visitors left, October 27, a baby girl was born to Elmer and Anna Mary Yoder, Mart and Susan's neighbors. They named her Rachel Irene. This was the first baby since Ida Ruth was born to Herman and Ida Yoder on May 20, 1985.

John Henry and Clara Stutzman and two boys came to live with Elmer and Anna Mary on October 29, to stay for a few weeks before going on to Texas to work on a dairy farm. Clara was a sister to Anna Mary and helped with the household duties.

Mart was making a set of harnesses for someone in his spare time. They were to be picked up on Wednesday, November 5. That day Susan watched as geese flew south all day. It was a nice sunny day and the sky seemed filled with the sound of geese. Snow and Canada geese were traveling together. That evening in the barn, Susan marveled at cow #5. Lula was mother to a new heifer calf. They were richly blessed.

On Sunday p.m., November 9, Elmer Yoders had company in the afternoon. Ben J. and Esther Troyer and Herman and Dorothy Stutzman and families came to see the new baby. In the evening the newlyweds, Abe and Lydia and Allen and Mary, came to see the baby too.

The next day Mart went to work for Elmer's construction crew again while Susan sewed harness pads in the harness part of the shop. Steven was making fence. As she worked she heard more geese going. She went to the door to look out and these geese were flying high and seemed to be in a real hurry. Cold weather must be setting in. Sure enough, the next morning they had frost on everything. Some of the low places had temperatures of 18-20 degrees. The fall gardens would now come to an end.

But it warmed up again after that, according to the letter Susan's sister Esta wrote to *The Budget* on November 17, 1986.

> Horses are sunning themselves in our 69° weather. It sure feels good compared to the 18° we had last Wednesday morning.
>
> We had green beans in the garden until then and others had lettuce, radishes, turnips, peas, and potatoes in their fall gardens yet. It is unusual to be that cold here the first part of November.
>
> Visitors over the weekend for communion were Bishop Dan Yoders from Delaware, Bishop Ben B. Troyers from Texas, and Minister Raymond Millers from Texas. Also passing through this weekend was Daniel B. Troyer on his way to Texas looking for work. Daniel is from Jamesport, Missouri.
>
> We had quite a wet experience picking up pecans the other week. Most owners let you pick up for half. The birds and squirrels get away with quite a lot of them. We used our small farm wagon to go pick up pecans about four miles from here and were caught in a rainstorm on the way home.
>
> Neighbor Winnie Patton is getting along well since having half of her left foot amputated. She is diabetic and gangrene had set in.
>
> Rachel Irene Yoder (Elmers) made her first appearance in church yesterday. She's bound to get lots of attention being the only wee one in the community, and

with three older brothers.

    Vernon E. Millers

Bishop Dan Yoders were parents of Andy Miller Mary, and Andys lived neighbors to Marts. Andys and Dans were both at the farm for supper one evening before going back to Delaware.

Susan sewed for the boys whenever she could. She made a new Sunday overcoat for Steven, and pants for Edwin. She also cut and sewed a little baby coat and cap for Elmers' new baby.

Susan was busy sewing and didn't hear a car drive up. It was after supper and chores when someone knocked at the door. Wondering who could be coming now, Susan opened the door and looked at a strange, yet familiar face. "I'm the deputy sheriff. Is Mr. Hochstetler in?" said the man, who wasn't wearing a uniform. It took a few minutes to soak in, then Susan said, "John Burdge! Is it really you? For a minute there, you almost had me scared. My, it's good to see you!"

That evening the boys sat wide-eyed as John began talking of bygone days. They talked of the trip when he moved Mart and Susan to British Columbia soon after their wedding day in May of 1970. All the different trips he made to Horsefly, British Columbia to bring family members to visit the ranch. The time he was rendering bear grease in the camper to the trip to Bella Coola on the coast and back to the ranch. The hairpin curves down the steep mountainside when Susan jumped out of the back of the camper and declared she would walk. Every time he came to the ranch he'd take a swim in the Horsefly River. He talked about the long journey back to home folks in Ohio when he moved them back. Steven was fifteen months old and John would do his share in helping to keep him occupied. Before they left the ranch in August of 1972, John made a point of swimming in the Horsefly River one more time. The hours flew by and soon it was midnight. When the clock struck twelve Susan jumped up from her chair and exclaimed, "Boys, it's high time to get to bed. Edwin has to go to school tomorrow and we have to get up at 4:00 to milk cows, don't forget." Reluctantly the boys went to bed after the evening prayer. As Edwin was leaving for bed he whispered to his mother. "Sure wish I could have been along on all that." "Maybe someday you can see Horsefly and the ranch. But now we better all get some sleep," replied Susan.

The next evening more visitors came to the farm. Lamar and Joanna Eash and daughter Laverda Ann had been to a wedding in Chouteau and came down from there. They were there for supper and overnight. They also visited late hours as Lamars had lived in the basement of Mart and Susan's house on the ranch in Rexford, Montana as newlyweds from Bloomfield, Iowa. After breakfast the next morning Lamars traveled on to their home in Bloomfield, Iowa. Joanna's two brothers were also along.

November soon passed, and now it was December and only a few weeks before Christmas. Mart got word that his mother would be coming for Christmas. Also his sister Kathy who lived on the home place with his mother. Kathy was married to Levi J. Schlabach. They would come bringing along their five children, Anna, Marty, Jonas, Miriam, and Adam. Mart's brother Atlee and family were planning on arriving in time for Christmas too. Atlee and two of the boys, Jacob and Joseph, had gone to Mexico by bus and were coming from there. His wife Drusilla and the rest were coming with Mom and Levis. They would all travel home together then with the van and Kenny Geiser as driver.

There was excitement on the farm as the days went by, and soon only a few more days were left until Christmas. It had been a long time since they had family for Christmas. This was special. Susan had some orders for Christmas cookies, so she needed to get them out of the way first before she could get the Christmas menu started. Susan's sister Esta and Mart's sister Kathy were friends and Vernons' three children were about the same age as Levis' three oldest children. So they made arrangements to spend the nights at Vernons.

Mart and Susan were busy getting ready, but weren't ready yet when Atlee and the two boys arrived. The next day the van load arrived with the rest from Ohio. Atlees' boys had grown up and were so tall and healthy looking. Ivan was twenty-one already, and Jacob nineteen, Joseph eighteen, Daniel seventeen, and Reuben sixteen. They brought sleeping bags and bunked in the red shanty. Susan tried to visualize sewing denim pants for six men instead of three men. These boys had all grown up to young men. You could buy denim material by the bolt and still have none left over. If they were growing spiritually as well as physically, that was a lot to be thankful for. Christmas was such a special time because of Jesus' birth and God's love for us was evident when He sent His only Son to be born in a lowly manger to grow up among the people, and then die on the cross for our sins. Then too, Christmas is family time when family gatherings are taking place in many homes. So this was very special to have family here, as it had been many years since they had this privilege. It was an enjoyable, happy occasion. Mart and Susan worked late to make small gifts for Atlees' boys and Levis' children.

Right after Christmas, on December 27, Lena (Mommy) Mast died. She had been ill for some time. She was Dan Mast's mother and a widow, and had lived at Dans. They had services in the Clarita settlement for her then took her to Kalona, Iowa for burial.

This marks the end of the second year at the Clarita settlement for Mart and Susan.

chapter six

The Third Year

NEW YEAR'S DAY 1987 BROUGHT COMPANY to the Hochstetlers. A load from Indiana stopped in on their way home from Texas. Mr. and Mrs. Homer Lee Miller, Loretta, Lyle, and Leon, Monroe and Mary Bontrager and son Steve, and Marlin and Erma Schrock with Claude Marner as driver had supper at Mart and Susan's place on New Year's. Homer was a brother to Leroy, sister Elizabeth's husband. It was nice to visit with them.

Several days later, neighbor Andrew Miller came to tell Susan that more company was coming. There was a message for them, and he conveyed the news. On January 3, another load stopped in to visit for awhile. Susan had just finished baking a batch of Ranger Joe cookies and passed them around to the visitors. On this load were Ben Jr. and Mary Troyer and daughters, Jolene, Jessica, and Bethany, Eli and Liz Glick, and Mrs. Anna Miller and two sons, Josie and Herman. Also Anna's married son Richard and wife and baby Kevin, with driver Edna Yoder. This load was also on their way home from Texas. Most of them were also from Topeka, Indiana. All except Ben Jr. and Mary and girls, who were from Sugarcreek, Ohio, as was driver Edna.

Ben Jrs. had stayed at Vernon and Esta's overnight and

for breakfast. Mary was kind of like a sister to Susan's family. Since she was married, she moved from Topeka, Indiana to Sugarcreek, Ohio amongst Junior's family. Junior's brother John was married to Susan's sister Mary Ellen, and Mary's brother Leroy was married to Susan's sister Elizabeth. So Elizabeth had moved to Indiana amongst Leroy and Mary Kay's family and they live on the home farm with Leroy's mother, Anna (a widow), who was also along on this trip. Mary Kay would often go home with Mary Ellen to Elmer and Katie's, thus Katie became like her "other mother." Now Katie, Susan's mother, was buried here in Oklahoma. It had all seemed rather unreal to Mary Kay as she wasn't able to come to the funeral. Now they could see where Elmer and Katie had lived in the little red shanty, and could go to the cemetery where she was buried.

All too soon the company had left and Susan had to get back to her duties. She needed to get back to work as the next day was butchering day at Andy Millers and she needed to get some things done before going to Andys.

The load of visitors had lifted her spirits and she sang happily as she went about her work. It was so wonderful how the good Lord worked through other people to answer your prayers. And it often came so unexpected.

The next day the neighbors gathered at Andy Millers to butcher their beef. While there Mart dressed Elmer Yoders' beef too, and so the neighbors gathered at Elmers several days later to work up and can their meat. Marts got some fresh beef. It was good to have meat on hand. In Montana they ate a lot of deer and elk meat. Beef was good but more greasy. You just had to trim all the fat and make it lean meat and it was good too.

The January days soon slipped into February, and by the last week in February the peach trees were already starting to bloom and spring was just around the corner. That meant the purple martins would soon be coming again. They needed to get their box ready.

Mart was in the shop part making a two-door grooming cabinet for someone who wanted to put it in their barn for grooming supplies.

Steven and Edwin were spending their evenings in the pigpen. The sows were starting to farrow and the weather had turned colder. One evening it was rainy, cold, and miserable. Mart had come in from the pigpen with a box full of squealing little newborn piglets. "Here," he told Susan. "Try to get these warmed up by the stove if you can." And he left to join the boys who were "pig-sitting".

Susan took the box of squirming, squealing little pigs and headed for the stove. She set the box down and grabbed an old blanket and took each piglet out of the box, one at a time, and rubbed it all over with an old towel, getting its cold, stiff body warm again, and then put it down on the old blanket right beside the stove which was crackling merrily and giving off an abundance of heat. There were ten little piglets and Mart had said three didn't make it, so the one mother pig had thirteen. That was a good-sized litter.

After the little piglets got warmed up by the stove they gave those satisfied grunts and soon dozed off to sleep. Mart came in to take them back out to their mother for their feeding. Warm milk from their mother did wonders to satisfy the gnawing hunger pains.

Mart and Susan took second shift so the boys could go to bed. Another sow had farrowed and now there were two mother pigs with ten piglets each.

About midnight, Mart and Susan left the pig stall to get some sleep before it was time to get up at four o'clock in the morning. All seemed well in the pigpen. This reminded Susan of calving time in Montana. She used to go with Mart twice or thrice during the night to check on the mother cows and baby calves.

Norman and Sylvia Miller and daughter Rachel were moving back into the Clarita settlement again. On February 25, Susan was up early to prepare the meat for sloppy joe sandwiches and to start the dough for the buns before going to the barn. She would be taking sandwiches for moving day. The neighbors at the north end all welcomed Normans back, as did the whole community. Susan had wished them a nice day, but it was raining that morning, so Normans had a very muddy moving day. The big semi which brought their belongings got stuck. They had to get someone with a winch truck to pull the semi out. The other truck pulling a trailer got stuck too. Mart went home to get his team of horses to pull that truck out of the ditch. Bob and Bruce did their job well, and the truck and trailer were able to go on.

By the time Susan went home, Normans were pretty well settled in their shop part of the barn. They had added on to that part so they had more room. They would live in that part until they had their house built and the basement ready to move in. Normans wanted to start on their house as soon as it dried off enough for the cement trucks to get in.

That evening Susan cooked corn mush for supper. The boys had done the milking as Susan was still at Normans when it was time to start milking.

After supper Mart went to Vernons to use Vernon's planer to plane some lumber. He had an order for wooden boxes for someone from Oklahoma City. He got these orders from people who came to the harness shop.

February was fast coming to a close. It was now four years February 15, that Grandpa Hochstetler, Mart's dad, passed away. So Susan wanted to be sure and write Mom Hochstetler again soon.

Susan had read in *The Budget* where a couple in Guys Mills had lost all four of their children in a house fire. That would be a tragedy indeed. She prayed for the couple although she didn't really know them. A house fire is bad enough when losing all or most of your possessions, but to lose all your children yet would be devastating. May God help them cope and go on.

The garden was plowed and it was time to plant garden in Oklahoma. But it was too wet to plant. Steven spaded a plot by the shop where Susan had planted annual flowers last year. He raked it and Susan planted some radishes, lettuce, and onion sets. It was not as wet against the shop. She decided to put in a few cabbage plants yet. She was getting hungry for fresh garden vegetables.

Mart had found out that the Stratford, Oklahoma area had severe ice storms. The people that had come to the harness shop were telling him how the trees and everything had such a thick coat of ice that telephone poles snapped like toothpicks and trees exploded, sounding like guns going off and the area looked like a war zone that had been bombed. People lost valuable pecan groves.

Susan thought how thankful they should be to have had just rain and not ice yet too. They sure haven't had a loss like that nor lost any children. That evening they went to bed with thankful hearts.

On Thursday and Friday, February 26 and 27, it was still raining. Thursday Susan baked a cake to take along to Ben J. Troyers for his birthday supper. On Friday evening they went to the schoolhouse as there was a singing there that evening.

Susan was quite excited about the latest news that her dad, Florida Dawdy, would buy Vernon and Esta's property in Clarita, and they would buy fifteen acres from Marts' east end of the farm and build a new carriage shop and house.

Neighbor Noah Coblentzs had visitors over the week-end, Noah Bylers and their married daughter and husband. Both men were ministers.

Elmer Yoders had gone to Canada to visit his parents and took baby Rachel along. Susan wanted to go check on Noah and Anna since Elmers were gone. Anna had been having back trouble.

The women in the community were taking turns to bake for teacher Edward Yoder. Susan wanted to bake a chocolate angel food cake for him.

The purple martins returned in March and the sun finally did shine again. The garden was planted and it was soon growing by leaps and bounds.

This year Lindy had a healthy stallion colt, the banty hen hatched another set of chicks, and new calves and baby pigs were everywhere. Another spring and the green grass was growing. Susan loved the springtime of the year. The birds were singing everywhere, and she felt like singing too.

Vernon and Esta started breaking ground for their new house in early May. There was another rainy spell and the process was going slow for awhile.

On May 15, Henry Kempf of Fresno, Ohio stopped by. He was traveling with a load from Middlefield, Ohio.

More visitors on June 17, Mart's uncle and aunt from Beaver Springs, Pennsylvania stopped by for a visit with their son Aden along. Morris Osmund was their driver. Emery and Mary Ann Weaver were so welcome at Mart and Susan's place. Mart was so glad to see his relatives. Emery wasn't too sure about the bellowing bull out in the pasture and Aden didn't hesitate to express his opinion. But Mart assured them both that if they stayed on this side of the fence, they'd be safe. Susan had baked fresh blackberry pie and enjoyed cooking for the visitors. They all went to Boggy Depot on a picnic and what an enjoyable time they had.

Soon the canning season was in full swing and the green beans were a good crop. The boys sometimes helped snap them in the evenings after the chores. The can shelves in the shop were filling up and Susan counted sixty-seven quarts green beans as she carried them to the shelves. The new potatoes in the garden tasted so good with dandelion gravy or wilted lettuce. Yumm! What a treat! Fresh cucumber salad was another thing which was so good on new potatoes, cubed and boiled with salt and butter.

Susan used lettuce from the garden instead of dandelion most of the time as the dandelion came too early for new potatoes. She fried about four or five pieces of bacon. She wasn't really supposed to eat bacon or greasy foods so she poured off the grease and used canola oil in the same pan, added flour—half cup or so. She never measured. Dash of salt—sugar to taste. Add Miracle Whip—half cup or so; stir until bubbles. Add milk until it's the right consistency. Cut up lettuce in a bowl; add hard-boiled eggs, sliced—four or so. Crumble bacon on lettuce and eggs; add hot gravy. Ready to serve on boiled potatoes mashed with fork. This was a family favorite no one tired of eating.

One morning out in the milk barn Herbie got too close to one of the cows, and she kicked him in the leg. With a yelp and a howl Herbie went under the feed bin. They were almost done milking. Once the cows were all through, Mart and the boys checked Herbie's leg and were quite sure it was broken. A trip to the vet confirmed that it was, so the poor Border collie came home with a cast on. He did not like the cast and that night he set to work getting rid of the bothersome thing the strange man had put on his leg. He chewed and tore and ripped until it all came off. Susan was concerned that he'd go on three legs now the rest of his life and not be able to enjoy his farm work. Herbie limped around for awhile, but it finally healed. Although he had a crooked leg, he went on all four legs and resumed his job in the milk barn. He was a go-getter, a fighter, and a very remarkable dog.

Mart was making preparations to build a new hay barn to put all their hay in. They had been putting it in a large stack, but lost some hay that way. He wanted to put a lean-to on the one side with a feed bunk to feed the cows hay during the winter months. They were getting more cows from a dairy that was selling out, so they needed more room for feeding.

Susan was busy that spring and summer with a project that took a lot of time. She was writing a book of their experiences and life on the ranch in British Columbia, Canada. They were working with Wayne Murphy of Faith Publishing House in Oklahoma to get it printed.

Florida Dawdy helped out at Vernons and Marts a lot that summer. He painted Marts' barn and the inside of the milk house. He also painted Vernons' house.

The last part of July Vernon and Norman helped Mart cement the lean-to of the new barn. The weather had been a little cooler during July and not so very warm day after day. Mart was hoping to get the barn finished for second cutting hay.

Steven had a rough summer with an appendectomy and infection following causing a lot of pain and discomfort. He was finally able to go back to hauling hay and both boys also helped Mart with a fencing job at the Braums Ranch with Bruce Norton.

With more cows to milk it took longer to do the milking, but with all four helping it could be done. The new cows did not get named, but went by numbers which were either on ear tags or chains around their neck. They all eventually had ear tags.

Steven had joined instruction class that summer and Susan went to Herman Stutzmans where Dorothy helped her with the mutza she was making for his baptismal suit. She could sew the jacket and pants, but she had never made a mutza before. Dorothy showed her how and Susan did the sewing.

The busy summer months went by quickly. Susan found a poem or prayer and copied it off and hung it above her sink so she could read it every day. She felt she needed that reminder in their busy schedule.

Lord, Remind Me
As we travel down the road of memory, there are

experiences, priceless and precious, that we should remember. Some were made in the valley, others on the hilltop, but experiences that have made us what we are.

When our children tug at our aprons, remind me, Lord, to be kind and patient. When our teenagers need attention, remind me, Lord, to take time to be kind and patient and explain, so that in years to come, no bitter memories shall fill our empty rooms.

When I sit down to the table laden with the bounty of the land, remind me, Lord, that half the world is hungry. Curb my appetite with the vision of a crying, starving child, begging for a crumb and getting nothing. When I get so engrossed with duties of the day, remind me that only that which is eternal and spiritual is important. I don't want to become calloused and thoughtless, but I so soon forget. So please, Lord, remind me of all this and give us a thankful heart.

Susan couldn't remember where she had found this or who wrote it, but it did her good to read it each day.

The first of September rolled around with Susan getting ready for church again. This time it was baptismal services and since their shop was rather small, they decided with Vernon and Esta's consent to have church in Vernons' new shop which was much bigger. The ones taking instructions all summer and now being baptized on September 6, 1987, were Jacob Stutzman, Mose Hershberger, Steven Hochstetler, Kathryn Miller, Roseanna Mast, and Heidi Yoder. They were baptized by Bishop Melvin Yoder of Chouteau, Oklahoma.

This was a very touching day for both Mart and Susan, and they hoped to be a good example, with God's help for their growing boys. Life was so short and eternity is forever. Eternity where? Where will we spend eternity? Lord, help us all to stay on the narrow road that leads to Heaven above. These were Susan's thoughts as the last hymn was sung and church was dismissed. Now she had to concentrate on getting the food on the table as soon as the men had set up the tables. They made tables with the church benches. Lunch consisted of homemade bread, peanut butter spread, cheese or meat for sandwiches with pickles and pickled red beets, tea, and coffee.

After lunch there was some time to visit with the visitors who had come for the baptismal services. There was a load from Chouteau, and one from Yoder, Kansas, and Jake Petersheims from Indiana. Jake was Herman Dorothy's uncle. He had the opening sermon, Noah Coblentz read the Scriptures, and Bishop Melvin Yoder had the main sermon and baptized them with Mart pouring the water. Yes, life was serious; it is no child's play. Only what we do for Christ will last.

By evening Susan had a slight sore throat. But she was thankful she felt well enough to keep going as there was supper to prepare and the hymn singing afterwards. Susan made cheese and lettuce sandwiches for supper as they had fresh lettuce in the fall garden. She had fixed a potato-hamburger casserole and the others brought in jello, pudding, and pie.

Mart's brother Ivan had stopped in on his way West and brought cheese and Trail bologna and a box with goodies from Grandma Hochstetler. Ivan had brought extra bologna and cheese and said Mart and Susan could use it for church. It was put to good use. The boys and Mart really enjoyed their Trail bologna and Swiss cheese in their lunch pail on their fencing job too. It was a real treat! Edwin was now out of school and ready to do other things besides school work. Although Susan had asked him to draw some pictures for the book, if she could corner him long enough to work on it. And write a poem too.

Sometimes people who came to the harness shop asked about the Amish faith. Mart was usually at work so Susan tried to explain that the basic doctrines of salvation as held by the Amish church are: Man is sinful (Romans 3:23) and needs to repent and be baptized (Acts 2:38), accepting by grace the atonement of Christ on the cross (Ephesians 2:8 and 9 and Romans 5:8). They teach that redemption goes hand in hand with discipleship and self-denial. The blood of Christ washes away our sins.

One man asked, "Why don't you have a car, but ride in a car?" "Well, we don't feel the car is evil itself, but feel the trend of life the car brings with it is not good for the family unit and structure of the Amish community."

One day a woman came to the shop and got some grooming supplies. She was rather hesitant at first but finally asked, "May I ask you why you wear that white bonnet (cap) on your head?" Susan tried to explain that Amish women wear a cap for a prayer covering in obedience to the Bible in I Corinthians 11:5 where it says, "Every woman that prayeth or prophesieth with her head uncovered dishonoreth her head." She went on to explain that Amish women don't cut their hair because of I Corinthians 11:6. We don't wear jewelry (read I Timothy 2:9 and 10 and I Peter 3:3 and 4). The woman seemed satisfied with that and left.

The next week Mart had a sore throat and couldn't talk loud. Susan had felt sick the day after baptismal church, but hitched up old George and went down to Vernons' carriage shop to bring back all the things that were left over from church. It was a beautiful sunny day and had been the day before for church too. Her throat felt better after gargling with warm salt water. In a few days she felt as good as new and was thankful for renewed strength.

That fall Mart started work on the new house. They would start, but didn't know how far they'd get. Ben J. Troyer and Bruce did the brick work after the frolics to frame it up and the cement work was done.

Mart's grandpa, Mart Hochstetler, died that week and Mart wasn't at home for the first frolic as he left to attend the funeral. Grandpa had been such a good Christian example for his children and grandchildren.

It wasn't until the spring of 1988 that the house was far enough along to move in. During the winter months Susan dreamed of their new house. Someday they would have a house. (Lord willing.)

Several days after Christmas, on December 27, 1987, Susan's two sisters and families came out to spend the week of Christmas and New Year's in Oklahoma with Marts and Vernons. It was a very enjoyable week. John and Mary Ellen and their six children and Leroy and Elizabeth and their five children. There was never a dull moment!

Susan was so glad to get out of the shop after being cramped in there for three years. There are worse things than that, but a house was such a blessing and really was appreciated.

Soon after they were in the new house they had visitors in May of 1988 from Holmes and Wayne County. Mart's brother Abe and wife Anna and their whole family with newly married daughter, Betty, and her husband, David Weaver, along. Then there was the Dannie Troyer family which was Mart's cousin Betty. They all stayed overnight and the next day yet. Marts sure enjoyed the visit. It was always so good to see family and relatives again.

The purple martins had new housing which Florida Dawdy had made to put up by the new house. He was back from Florida again and helped both Esta and Susan with outside work in the yard. He lived in his house in Clarita, but spent much time with Marts and Vernons.

The garden was planted for another year, but this year the rains were not so plentiful and the garden did not produce as well.

The drought of 1988 was quite severe and the pastures turned brown and the crops dried up. There was still green grass on the 250-acre lease Marts had on the Lee place down by the Boggy Creek. Each morning they would take the cows all the way over there so they could graze and in the evening bring them back. Susan enjoyed the walk but was tired by the time she got back.

That summer in July they had surprise visitors from Conewango Valley, New York, who came on the Greyhound bus, Mr. and Mrs. Mose E. Miller and Mr. and Mrs. Uria Miller. Mose's wife Mary Ann was a first cousin to Susan's mother and their daughter Clara and Susan were good friends and grew up together and went to school together. In Holmes County they were better known as Becky Mosa. What a pleasant surprise! Florida Dawdy and Vernons came to see the visitors too and the good old days of their youth were the main subject. When they all lived in the same church (Holmesville area in Ohio), went to the same school, and then just as Clara was about sixteen or seventeen they moved to New York State. For many years Susan's family had not seen them. So they had a lot to catch up on. Their visit came to an end all too soon. They left to catch the bus and were on their way again.

The summer sun shone clear and bright day after day and no rain in sight. Finally even the creek beds dried up and the pastures beside the Boggy came to an end.

September was very busy with getting ready for the first school consignment sale at Vernon and Esta's new carriage shop. Esta had invited Bernice Schlabach of Fort Worth, Texas to come to the sale. She was Uncle Wesley's wife. He had passed away in 1972. Susan had hardly ever seen Wes and his family. They had two sons, Dannie (Robert Daniel) and Jack Paul. Jack had come with Bernice the day of the sale. They had Dannie's two sons along, named Eli Wesley and Andrew Daniel. Eli had just turned fifteen and Andrew was three years younger.

Steven and Edwin took the two boys up to the farm after the sale and showed them the milk barn and how the cooling tank worked in the milk house. This was something new to them. It was nice to see them and get acquainted with them after so many years.

October brought fall weather and the decision to sell the dairy herd and get beef or stocker cattle. This was a major decision, but finally the day came when a large semi pulled in and a lot of the cows went to Texas. Ora Hochstetler bought ten and the others went elsewhere. Thus the milk barn stood empty and no one had to get up at 4:00 in the morning. The boys were happy about that.

That fall Mart and Edwin went on the pecan harvest and Steven worked on a ranch. Susan was busy getting information together for a second book. The first book was selling well and already on its second printing. Susan was busy with book orders too. She kind of missed the cows and milking time, but she was too busy to think about it much. She needed to sew for Mart and the two boys. She had sent for a bolt of denim. She sewed a new denim overcoat for each of them and denim pants. Susan liked to sew pants for the men better than clothes for herself. The treadle sewing machine hummed day after day for awhile. Then Susan went back to writing again.

For several years now, Penny, the blind Pomeranian which Marts had brought to Oklahoma from Montana, was buried on the east edge of Marts' farm. Then a neighbor gave Edwin a puppy and it died several months later. So Mart got a little Chihuahua which Edwin named Trapper.

Trapper was a good little dog and devoted to the family. He enjoyed being outside too and was housebroken and trained well.

Susan started baking to sell that fall and was busy baking one day when Trapper went to the door and barked, so Susan opened the door and let him out. She went on with her baking and decided she'd better check and see why he hadn't scratched on the door to come in again. She called and called, but no Trapper. After her pies were out of the oven she went out to call again. She checked the ditches beside the road and called and called again. That evening the boys went to search in earnest. But Trapper was gone.

Susan was beginning to think maybe they shouldn't get another dog. She often wondered if maybe a coyote had gotten Trapper. Or maybe a hawk had carried him away. Maybe someone picked him up out by the road and stole him. Or maybe someone ran over him and took him away so they wouldn't have to see him. No one knew, nor would they ever find out.

Marts were at the Texas flea market one Saturday after Trapper disappeared. They got a fox terrier puppy which they called Tootsie. She was not trained or taught anything. A tiny weanling, she needed a lot of teaching and time to grow. But she stayed with the family for many years.

Susan had canned very little from the garden that year because of the drought. But she had canned 127 quarts of pears, so they would have at least that. They wouldn't butcher until after New Year's, so she found ways to cook a meal without much meat. They bought some and got some canned goods from a salvage store. They would make out. The Lord had always provided. They still had plenty to eat. Just not the usual stocked shelves of canned goods they were used to having each fall.

Mart was doing dozer work for Bob Weed on his ranch. Bob wanted to build a pond and stock some fish and also use it as a stock tank for the cattle. He worked many days until he was completely finished.

Susan sometimes went over to the ranch to spend some time with Bob's wife, Delores. But she didn't have much spare time with writing another book, sending book orders of the first book, and baking rolls, bread, pies, and such to sell.

During December more visitors came to the farm. Dan

and Iva Yoder (Mart's aunt) of Independence, Iowa came to visit. Their son and his wife, Atlee and Edna, were along too with their little baby Alma. They were from Ontario, Wisconsin. A nice visit and all too soon they too were gone again.

Soon December was gone and another Christmas was history. Now this marked the end of the third year and fourth summer for Mart and Susan on their farm in Oklahoma. Come April of 1989 it would be four years. They did not know what the future would hold for them, but they know who holds the future.

Mart and Susan decided to sell the farm in Oklahoma and once more move closer to home folks. They had a farm auction on November 23, 1991, and moved to West Union, Ohio the first week in December 1991. At the time of this writing (2003) they still live in the West Union area.

On the following page is the sale bill for their auction in Oklahoma.

AMISH FARM AUCTION
SATURDAY, NOVEMBER 23 • 10:30 A.M.
CLARITA, OKLAHOMA

Sale Location: From Tupelo, go 6 miles South on Hwy. 48, turn east, go 1/2 mile. From Wapanucka: Go 10 miles North on Hwy. 48, turn east, go 1/2 mile to Auction Site. WATCH FOR AUCTION SIGNS

OWNERS: MR. AND MRS. MARTIN HOCHSTETLER

NOTE: Mr. and Mrs. Hochstetler have decided to quit their farming operation and move to Ohio. They have commissioned Lawrence Auction Service to sell at Public Auction the following farm equipment, hay, and miscellaneous items, to the highest bidder with NO MINIMUM or reserve bids.

EQUIPMENT

1- New Holland 258 hay rake
1- John Deere 336 hay baler, twine tie
1- MF 33 grain drill, 15 hole
1- Gehl grinder mixer
1- New Holland E-Z flow
1- John Deere Manure spreader
1- International 16 hay rake (for parts)
1- Two-bottom horse drawn breaking plow
1- Three-section harrow
1- Lister 4 cyl. diesel power unit, 31 hp. with PTO
1- 18 ft. square bale elevator
1- Running gear for cotton wagon

1- Three-section spring harrow
1- 9 ft. Culti packer
1- Overhead bulk feed bin, approx. 16 ton
1- Pioneer walking plow
1- 16 ft. flatbed wagon
1- John Deere sickle mower, 7 ft. cut
1- One- cylinder gas engine with reduction gear
1- Fishtail riding cultivator
1- McCormick Deering H/D sickle mower, 7 ft. cut
1- Cherokee pop-up hay loader
1- 8 ft. Horse-drawn disk
1- Old Grain binder

MISCELLANEOUS EQUIPMENT

Platform cotton scales, 8 ft. x 14 ft.
12- 16 ft. tubular cattle panels
6 1/2 ft. x 28 ft. hay bunk
Several feed troughs, 8 hole hog feeder
4- Round bale feeders
3- Steel watering tanks
Loading chute
Power Kraft jointer, table saw
2- Rolls barbed wire, several T-posts

Trailer house axle
Diesel hand pump
Steel wheels, stainless wash vat
Dehorners, ear tagger, nose tongs, cow kickers
Calf pullers
2- push type lawn mowers
1- Reel type push mower
Scrap iron, pitch forks, garden tools
2- car garage door (wood)

HAY & OATS

1960- Square bales Hay grazer
720- Square bales bean hay
500- Square bales wheat and Johnson grass
2020 -Square bales wheat and rye
60- Round bales Bermuda and Johnson grass
Approximately 12,000 lbs. oats

HORSES & BUGGY

1- 10 yr. old Quarter mare sorrel with blaze face, broke to ride or drive
1- 18 mos. old 1/4 Percheron, 3/4 Arabian bay filly
4- Sets draft work harness
2- Horse feeders
2-Wheel breaking cart
2- Seated spring buggy
3 & 4 Horse eveners
Hames, single trees, collars and tack

FURNITURE AND APPLIANCES

Ashley wood heater
Vesta gas cook stove
3-Burner kerosene stove
Maytag washing machine
Square rinse tubs
2- Sofas
2- Hide-a-beds
Ottoman
Vinyl chair on coasters

Black vinyl chair
Swivel rocker
Desk chair
Glass top end table
Canister set
Tupperware
Ice cream freezer
PLUS LOTS OF MISCELLANEOUS

Owner or Auction Service Will Not Be Responsible for Theft or Accidents
Announcements Day of Sale Supercede All Advertising
CONCESSIONS AVAILABLE

Sale Conducted by
DON LAWRENCE - AUCTIONEER
LAWRENCE AUCTION SERVICE
Rt. 5 Box 1115, Coalgate, Okla. 74538 • Phone 405-428-3418

The Years of 1990 & 1991

F OLLOWING ARE LETTERS SUSAN WROTE TO
The Budget in 1990 and 1991 of community events. After the tragedy in February of Rachel Sue Miller (Normans),
the community was very saddened and needed the prayers
of others to help Norman and Sylvia go on without their
only child. Rachel had died in an accident on the way to
school one morning when a grain truck hit the children.
More on the accident in Part II under Norman's story.

1990 Coalgate, Oklahoma

March 26—We had more rain again yesterday with ice
covering the trees and fences. The purple martins are returning and seem rather bewildered.

I'm writing this at the Mason Medical Clinic in Atoka.
We brought our son Steve in to see the doctor. He's been
sick for about a week now and isn't getting much better. We
had taken him to the Coalgate Hospital emergency room
last Wednesday eve. He was treated for infection and told
he had the flu. The medication given hasn't brought any re-
sults, so we came here to further check out the problem.

We just now discovered, after running tests on blood
samples, that it's a good chance he has Rocky Mountain tick
fever. This can be treated if taken care of properly. There is

also a possibility of walking pneumonia. He is on different antibiotics now.

Allen Jay Miller might be coming home from Valley View Regional Hospital tomorrow. His mother stayed with him on Sunday; his brother Andrew spent Saturday night with him and sister Kathryn was with him Friday night.

Joe Masts have started milking part-time for the Nelsons' dairy.

Norman Millers had company for dinner on Sunday. Their guests brought dinner along. They were Sylvia's brothers and sister, Perry Lee and Marvin Yoders and families, and Ruth and Gary Yoder, all of Chouteau, Oklahoma. Ruth and Gary are published to be married April 5.

We were to Norman's a little while on Sunday evening. Norman's brother Glen was also there. He plans to start for Ohio tomorrow. He has been here since the funeral. He did the chores at Normans' today as they and Robert Millers went to Chouteau for the day to help with Daniel Yoder's basement house at Nelson Yoder's. John Henry, Reuben and Mary Miller were at Norman's this evening to visit Glen yet before he left for Ohio.

Norman and Sylvia have had company almost every evening which they appreciate. Also the many cards and letters of encouragement which they still receive.

Hopefully, we will plant garden tomorrow. Quite a few others have planted theirs in between the rains.

Winter wheat and rye pastures are doing well with all the wet weather, but we also need sunshine now and warmer temperatures to give things a boost.

Someone left a shawl at Norman's the day of the funeral, also a child's blue coat. They haven't been claimed yet.

April 2—The sun has been shining the last couple days with temperatures going up to 80°. Weatherman says we had over twenty-five inches of rain since the rains began about two months ago. The local ranchers say it's the wettest spring they've seen in years.

Our state bird, the scissor-tailed fly-catcher, can be seen along the roadside perched on fences or wire lines. It is a beautiful bird, pale pearly gray with an extremely long scissor-like tail. The sides and wing linings are salmon pink.

Steve will be going back to see the doctor on Wednesday. We took him to the hospital emergency in Atoka on Friday evening. He had severe stomach pains. This is something which accompanies the fever. Rocky Mountain spotted fever can last five or six weeks. Steve has been sick two weeks now. The doctor said it's just been twelve years or so that they really know how to treat this.

Church was at Dan Masts'. To be there again in two weeks. Sunday evening visitors here with us were the Andy Miller family and Noah and Anna Coblentz. Allen Jay and Malinda came along with Andys. Malinda had a new cast put on her leg. She gets around fairly well. She and Allen Jay were both in church Sunday.

Mrs. Herman Yoder and daughter Ruth and Mrs. Abe Hershberger and children spent Thursday with Mrs. Norman Miller. Norman and Sylvia left this morning for her parents' home in Chouteau. They want to help with preparations for the upcoming wedding of Sylvia's sister Ruth on April 5th. On Tuesday (April 3) they want to attend a hospital aid meeting in Kansas.

The schoolgirls from Elm Creek School visited Malinda

Miller last Wednesday evening and stayed the night in honor of her birthday. The next evening the neighbors reminded Mary, Malinda's mother, of her birthday. Both are on the same day.

We have had many letters asking us what Oklahoma really looks like. That all depends on who you talk to and in what part of Oklahoma you go. Here in our settlement the land is from flat to rolling. Some of our people have dairies. This is also cattle country with many of the local old-timers having ranches. Some people say this is the land of extreme. When it's wet, it's very wet, and when it's dry, it's very dry. The southeastern corner close to the Arkansas line has yellow pine forests, with logging operations in full swing.

We enjoy the short winters. We don't need large barns or loafing sheds to keep our cattle during the winter. The winter grazing on wheat and rye pastures beats feeding hay all winter long, although we do feed hay during the coldest weather.

April 9—Cloudy and on the cool side. Temperature 65°. There are tornado warnings out for the northern part of the state.

We just got back from Doctor's Park in Ada, where we had taken Steve to see a specialist. They took more tests. Our doctor in Atoka sent us there. He had arranged for the appointment. We won't get the reports of the tests until late tomorrow. Steve feels a little better but is still very weak.

Last week three young folks from West Union, Ohio arrived at Raymond Millers'. They were Eddie Yutzy, Joe Schmucker, and Kathryn Yoder. Their driver went on to Tyler, Texas to visit relatives. The West Union young folks, along with Susan, Mary, John Henry, and Reuben Miller, were here Tuesday evening to visit Steve.

The above named all went to Stephenville, Texas, on Wednesday, coming back Thursday p.m.

Mark Hershbergers of Kalona, Iowa visited with their daughter and family, the Robert Millers several days last week. Their driver took the load to Stephenville then.

Last Wednesday Herman Yoders and two daughters Lori and Ruth, Mrs. Abe Hershberger and children left for Chouteau attending the wedding at Levi Yoders' on Thursday. Allen Yoders and Freeman Yoders left for the same wedding early Thursday morning. Both loads came home Thursday evening again.

Andy Millers had a pleasant surprise on Friday evening when supper was brought in by Herman Stutzmans, Herman Yoders, Joe Masts, Ora Hochstetlers and Raymond Millers. Most of the young folks were there, too, including the three from West Union.

Elmer Yoder's constructions crew had a farewell supper at Elmers' Saturday evening for Edward Yoders. Those present were Andy Millers, Freeman Yoders, Norman Millers, both of the drivers David, and Homer and their families, the four of us and the guests of honor, Edward Yoders. We took Steve home soon after supper.

Edwards will be moving to Ludington, Michigan in two weeks.

Sunday afternoon visitors with us were Noah and Anna Coblentz and some young folks. Supper and singing was at Dan Masts'.

April 16—Thundershowers on Easter Sunday with a tornado watch for the Clarita area. The south end of our community had about three inches of rain with hail, but Clarita had golf ball size hail.

Our community has had a lot of activity the past week with a quilting at Dan Masts' last Tuesday for Edward Yoders' two quilts, the one being a farewell gift from the community, the other a top Ruby's grandmother Lena had pieced. On the eleventh the Elm Creek School had their picnic day. The four pupils who graduated from eighth grade this year were Tobias Yoder, Esther Hershberger, Miriam Stutzman and Cindy Miller. A game of softball was enjoyed by young and old in the afternoon.

At Norman Millers' on Friday p.m. were Susan, Mary, John and Reuben Miller. The young folks and Vernon Millers were all here on Friday evening to see Steve, bringing a sunshine box along. He is gaining some and eats better. He was able to be in church awhile on Sunday. We have an appointment with his doctor in Atoka again tomorrow. Since the young folks were all here anyway on Friday evening, we served cake and ice cream in honor of Edwin's seventeenth birthday.

Church was at Dan Masts' yesterday with Ben B. Troyers of Stephenville, Texas present. Mrs. Levi B. Troyer and two children came along with Bens and spent Saturday p.m. and night at her parents', the Raymond Millers. She and the children also attended church. Next church services to be at Ben J. Troyers'.

Tomorrow, the seventeenth, is moving day for John Henry Stutzmans. They bought a property here and are moving from Sulphur Springs, Texas. Elmer Yoder's carpenter crew was remodeling John Henry's house and adding several new rooms. Bruce Troyer is making the cabinets.

Elmer Yoder has had two crews going for the most part of this last year. Our son Edwin is helping the crew which is working on a log house northeast of Coalgate. This is a large three-story house with 7,500 square feet, including the porches. Elmer started this job in November. It took ten men and a crane three and a half days to set up all the logs which arrived from Victor, Montana on four different trucks. Most of the logs were forty-four feet long and had been assembled before being hauled here. This house has over 22,000 board feet of 2 x 6 tongue and grove for the ceilings and floors. The roof is a five V crimp colored metal. The basement is poured concrete.

Melvin Hershbergers are building a larger store for their bulk foods and baked goods. Ben J. Troyer is helping with the building.

April 24—We had several days of sunshine after seven inches rain this last week. The river bottoms were flooded again. The purple martins should be well supplied with mosquitoes this year with all the water in the ditches and puddles in the fields.

Edward Yoders loaded their belongings Saturday and started for Ludington, Michigan early Monday morning, with Nem Wafford as driver, pulling a cattle trailer.

Another load started north early Monday morning with C.L. Dueck as van driver. Passengers on that load were Dan Masts and two girls, Rosanna and Wilma, Andy Millers and three children, Steven, Kathryn and Allen Jay. They had plans to stop in Arthur, Ill. to visit Andy J. Mast (Andy Miller's nephew) and Andy E. Mast (Verna Mast's brother). Both Andy Masts live close neighbors. The Andy Miller family (except Steven) plan to attend the wedding of Monroe Miller (Jonas) and Mary Yoder (Eli) at Wautoma, Wisc. The Dan Mast family and Steven Miller will travel on to Ludington, Mich. where they expect to help Edward Yoders get settled in their new home.

Joe Masts left last Monday with Bobby Bears as driver on a two-week trip. Their first stop was at Joe's sister in Garnett, Kansas. Tobias Yoder went along and stayed at his grandparents' for the week. Joes then traveled on to Jamesport, Mo. to visit friends and relatives.

Malinda Miller (Andys) is staying with the Herman Yoder family while Andys are on their trip. Andrew, Amos and John will try their luck at housekeeping while Andys are gone.

A load of young folks from here spent the weekend in Garnett, Kansas, starting Saturday morning and coming back Monday evening. They stopped at points of interest on the way back Monday. Earl Ray Chupp of Chouteau was their driver. Tobias Yoder traveled back with them.

Vernon Millers and children were here Sunday p.m. to visit Steve and stayed for supper. Steve was to see the doctor in Atoka last Tuesday. With further blood tests they have diagnosed his sickness as Kawasaki's syndrome, a disease very similar to Rocky Mountain spotted fever, with many of the same symptoms. A certain percent of the people who have Kawasaki's also have a heart defect, or problems with the tiny blood vessels around the heart. But a test taken with a specialist in Ada showed good news, so his heart wasn't affected. He is recovering and enjoys the many cards and letters he receives. It will be three to four weeks before he will be able to go back to work like normal. Kawasaki's is usually found in smaller children; Steve's case was rare.

May 1—We had another seven inches of rain since our last letter. Weather has been unsettled all week except for Saturday and Sunday we had beautiful sunny days with temperature in the eighties. This cool and rainy weather is unusual for our area this late in the spring. Easter weekend it stormed and hailed. Melvin Hershbergers had a lot more hail then they've ever seen before and larger than golf balls.

Church visitors at Ben J. Troyers' on Sunday were Minister Floyd and Betty Schrock and three sons, Nathan, Enos and Elvan and Mrs. Merle (Anna Mae) Bontrager and daughter Mattie. This load was from Haven, Kansas. From Sulphur Springs, Texas (Pickton) were Harvey and Wilma Troyer and three children, Mrs. Danny Joe Gingerich (Polly) and two daughters, and Nora M. Hershberger. Bobby Bears was their driver. Anna Mae and daughter spent Sunday p.m. and overnight at Herman Stutzmans'. She is a sister to Dorothy. Polly spent Sunday p.m. and evening at Joe Masts'. She is Mary's sister. Floyds spent Sunday night at Herman Yoders'. On Monday forenoon Hermans accompanied them through the back roads of Johnson County to deliver some wheels to a non-Amish farmer. Floyds had brought the wheels along Saturday evening, pulling a trailer behind the van. Their driver is in a wheelchair due to an accident while he was working for the silo company putting up silos. He gets around quite well. Floyds were here for dinner Monday, then left for Kansas around 1:15. They gave us a firsthand account of the tornado that went through Haven in March.

Visitors at Norman Millers' on Sunday p.m. were Harvey Troyers, Floyd Schrocks and Raymond Millers. Harvey also stopped at John Henry Stutzmans' awhile Sunday p.m., Johns' new address is Route 5, Box 67, Coalgate, OK 74538.

The purple martin population is quite high at Ben J. Troyers'. James has made and put up the third martin house. He takes good care of the birds and the bees, along with his other farm chores. They served some super good honey in church on Sunday.

Esther Troyer (Ben) had quite a lot of stomach pain Friday and Saturday. She took a trip to Durant to see her doctor Saturday just before they had church. Doctor thought it came from problems connected with the gallbladder. She was better Sunday.

The young folks reminded David Stutzman on Thursday evening that he is twenty one years old now. A volleyball game was enjoyed and pizza and ice cream was served. Steve was able to go for the first time since he's been sick. He was also in church Sunday and stayed for supper and singing for the first time in quite awhile. He still tires easy, but is slowly gaining strength.

We will try and answer some of your questions about Kawasaki's. No, it's not in the medical books unless you have a very recent one. This has just been a recent discovery by a Japanese doctor, named Kawasaki. Thus, the disease was named after him. It is much more common in Japan, but also more cases found in California than other states. This does not come from a tick bite, but acts the same as R. M. spotted fever in the first two weeks of the illness. High fever, chills, severe headache, then the rash appears about the sixth day. Steve's hands and feet peeled. Gobs of skin came off. This was about the third week. This plus a blood test showing the high white cell count the third week was what made the doctor check further to see if it's Kawasaki's. This illness can clot the tiny blood vessels; that's why he has to take one pill a day for blood thinner. He also takes liquid nutrition which has a lot of B vitamins to help get his strength back and soon now the white cell count should be going down.

He wasn't in the hospital anytime except for the two times in the emergency room. The tests he took in Ada at the specialists' were done at the clinic.

May 7—We have appreciated three days of sunshine after a very rainy week and high water. Last Tuesday and Wednesday we had another eight inches of rain. Some ranches east of us reported twelve inches during that time. By Wednesday evening the Boggy River started rising fast and by Thursday morning the Clarita area was surrounded by water. Route 48 and 31 were both flooded. On Highway 31 the Boggy flooded the bottomland and rose up over the new bridges, rising four feet above the road. On Highway 48 the water rose up over the bridge and reports were it was four feet above the road there, too.

After five o'clock Thursday morning no one could travel out and no one could come in except those going south toward Texas on Highway 48. Our little road was flooded east of us just at the edge of Vernon Millers' property. The flood control dam was backing up, plus the creek roaring in, and our neighbor who lived next to it said it was higher than a man where it crossed the road.

Our wheat and rye fields on our lease were completely flooded. You could row a boat over them. They are north of us next to the river. Our fescue field was also flooded. In some places you could see the tops of the fence posts. Fences are greatly damaged and some places completely out. This is the fourth time in a month that the Boggy spilled over its banks. This last time was worse than before.

Some ranchers took boats to check on their cattle who were stranded. Reports were a rancher south of here lost a herd of cattle in the floodwaters. The smaller creeks go down faster than the river. By Friday traffic was back on the highways again.

Mrs. Vernon Miller had a quilting last Thursday, with the quilt and wall hangings to be sold at the school auction this fall. Some buggies had to detour because of high water, but a good many came despite the circumstances.

Sunday dinner guests at Andy Millers' were Herman Stutzmans, Noah Coblentzes, Andy Miller Srs. of Delaware, Amos Mast of Delaware and the writer and family. Afternoon callers at Andys' were Vernon Millers and Ben J. Troyers. The Millers and the Masts came back from their trip to Wisconsin and Michigan Wednesday evening, just before the roads flooded. Andy Srs. plan to spend the week at Andys', then travel on to Kentucky and Delaware.

Dinner was brought in at Norman Millers' Sunday by a load from Sulphur Springs, Texas. On the load were Harvey Troyers and two children, Andy Bylers and four children, Paul Kinsingers and Albert Wengerds and daughter. Elmer Yoders and John Henry Sutzmans were also at Normans for dinner. They furnished supper for the Texas load at Johns'.

Bobby Bears furnished transportation. They made a call at Andys' before going to Johns'. Dan Masts were p.m. callers at Normans'.

Melvin Hershbergers moved into their new store on Thursday evening. Joe Masts had open house, serving free coffee and doughnuts on Saturday at their dry goods store.

Malinda Miller had her cast taken off today and has to wear a splint for awhile. She was happy to see her family again.

Steve is still gaining. We have another appointment at the doctor's next week. They have to keep checking his white cell count.

Work on Elmer Yoder's new basement house has started. Norman Miller will be making the forms for the concrete walls and will do the cement work. Robert Miller is helping him. Ben J. Troyer and son Bruce will do the plumbing.

Usually the haying season would have started already. But this year most of the farmers couldn't get in the fields to fertilize. By now the wheat or rye has headed out, what's left of it, and it's still too wet to get in. But with the sun and wind we're having now it should dry out fast.

The wedding of Edwin Miller and Esther Troyer will be here at the Ben B. Troyer farm where Noah Coblentzes live. Those of you who plan to come from out-of-state, we welcome you to our homes as overnight guests. It's been quite a while since we had a wedding in this community.

Twenty years ago today, a young man took his new bride to start a new "Life on the Edge of the Wilderness."

May 15—Windy and partly sunny with temperature in upper 80s. The fields that weren't flooded two weeks ago are dried off enough to work up.

The men are getting ready to sow hay grazer this morning. Four horses in the drill. They want to try and hitch the packer behind the drill.

No hay making for us this spring. We grazed our winter wheat here on our farm. The wheat on our lease was claimed by the flood.

Church services were held at Ben J. Troyers Sunday the thirteenth (Mother's Day). Supper and singing also there in evening. Next services to be at Andy Millers'.

Quilting is to be here at our place Thursday, the seventeenth. Two more quilts for the school sale this fall.

Steve had his checkup at the doctor's today and his cell count is back to normal. His illness lasted two months. He still can't work a full day without resting. The doctor gave me some literature on Kawasaki's. So next week I hope to give a report on it.

May 21— Weather has been unsettled with tornadoes in the northern part of the state. We have had some very nice sunny days, though, and cool nights.

The men are sowing hay beans. Some of the farmers were making hay the past week. Not everyone has hay to make.

We were Sunday dinner guests at the Joe Mast home. Others also invited were Vernon Millers, Norman Millers, Noah Coblentzes, Dan Masts, Freeman Yoders, Raymond Millers and Mrs. Levi (Lovina) Troyer and two children of Stephenville, Texas.

Mrs. Ben B. Troyer and daughter Esther (bride-to-be) arrived in Atoka on the bus Thursday, the seventeenth, and will be here getting ready for the wedding on the thirty-first. Lovina Troyer and children traveled with them and are staying at her parents'. She is also helping with preparations for the wedding.

To those who inquired, yes, we are in Armadillo territory. They come out at night like raccoons. They have strong claws which they use to dig tunnels and burrows in the ground. They eat insects, earthworms, and snails, etc. They root up the ground. Sometimes you get up in the morning and declare that the neighbor's pigs had gotten out and rooted up the yard or garden. But instead it was an armadillo. The armadillo's shell is its best protection. The shell is made up of many small plates of hard bony armor fitted closely together. It is jointed across the back, allowing the animal to curl up in a tight ball with its head and tail tucked in out of harm's way. They usually use their shell as the last resort. They dig so fast, they often try to dig themselves rapidly into the ground when danger approaches.

Vernon Miller's two dogs team up to fight and kill armadillos. Tiny, a little rat terrier, hangs on to the tail while Tara, a husky chow, fights at the head.

Today is Steve's nineteenth birthday. He is almost back to normal. He was helping with the seeding and working cattle, dehorning, etc.

Melvin Ray Millers of Stephenville, Texas have bought Vernon Miller's property. Melvin Ray will use Vernon's shop for his cabinet and furniture business. Vernons plan to move to Ohio in September, or possibly before the fall school term starts.

We have been getting many letters asking about our third book (about Montana). Work on the book has come to a halt for the last three months. Writing books does not come first; we work on that when other work is not pressing. We won't be able to have it ready until November to December at the earliest, maybe not until the first part of next year.

May 28— Sunny skies after a stormy night on Saturday night. We had high winds and hail, but no damage done.

Church services were at Andy Millers' yesterday.

Thursday dinner guests at Joe Masts' were Melvin Hershbergers, Andy Millers, Herman Stutzmans, Herman Yoders, Ben J. Troyers, Elmer Yoders, Melvin Yoders of Chouteau and Ora Hochstetlers.

Melvin Yoders and Levi Yoders arrived in the area from Chouteau on the twenty-second. Levis visited with Norman Millers (their daughter) and Melvins were at Herman Yoders', which is their daughter. They stayed until Thursday.

On Thursday forenoon another load from Chouteau arrived at Norman Millers' bringing Sylvia's brothers and sister and families.

On Thursday p.m. the young folks came here for an afternoon of softball. We served pizza and ice cream in honor of Steve's nineteenth birthday. Also included in the birthday celebration were Andy and Andrew Miller.

We are now in Oklahoma City at the Children's Hospital. Herman Yoders' five-year-old daughter Ruth was taken to Oklahoma City Hospital by Life Flight this p.m. due to head injuries received from an accident at their farm. The three youngest girls were playing out behind the barn on an old piece of machinery. Ruth was hit in the head by a part that fell down and Claire had both big toes cut and mashed. A neighbor took Hermans and Ruth to Coalgate emergency where Oklahoma City Life Flight was notified.

Ruth was unconscious from the start. But just now at 11:30 p.m. Ruth is responding some by moving her arms and legs a little, and seems to want to talk, so that's good news.

Howard Nelson, the Coalgate banker, and his wife brought Herman and Ida up here after the helicopter took off. Bill Vineyard brought Herman Stutzmans, Andy Millers and Mart and me up. Bill and Herman Stutzmans are staying for the night. Andys and we are going home with the Nelsons.

Following is the report on Kawasaki syndrome (mucocutaneous lymph node syndrome), an apparently new syndrome described by a Japanese physician: In an effort to confirm the diagnosis, five of the six major things described should be present. 1. High fever may be present five or more days before the disease is manifested and may last for one to two weeks. 2. A rash appears after six or seven days. 3. Hands and feet get sore and skin starts to peel off in large amounts; this may vary. 4. Infected pharynx, dry fissured lips and a strawberry tongue. 5. Lumps appear along the lymph nodes. 6. Clotting of the tiny blood vessels around the heart.

Severe abdominal pain may occur. The white blood cell count is usually elevated. A slight anemia is present.

Kawasaki syndrome can be fatal if untreated. Since the symptoms of this disease are similar to other diseases, it can be difficult to make a correct diagnosis before the development of severe coronary involvement.

Treatment of K.S. has not been established, although the director of infectious diseases at the Children's Hospital in Denver said it does respond to intravenous immune globulin therapy if given within ten days.

This disease progresses through three stages: The acute stage (1-14 days) sub-acute stage (14-25), chronic stage (up to 60 days). K.S. is found mostly in young children.

May 30—The neighborhood is busy with the preparations for the wedding on Thursday. The rest of the Ben B. Troyer family arrived early Monday morning to help.

We arrived home from Oklahoma City Hospital at 3:00 last night. Ruth has shown some improvement. The rest of Herman's family and Sylvia Miller might go up to the hospital today.

June 4—Temperature in lower 90s. We had high winds Friday night and a large limb from our big hackberry tree by the shop blew off. It has dried off enough from our recent rains to work in the fields again.

The wedding of Edwin Miller and Esther Troyer brought many out-of-state guests to this community. Around 225 were served the noon meal at the Ben B. Troyer residence. Wedding church was at Vernon Miller's buggy shop. Anfang by Vernon Coblentz (Milroy, Ind.) scripture read by Joe Gingerich (Texas) and main sermon by John Detweiler (Marion, Ky.) Marriage vows were asked by Ben B. Troyer (father of the bride). Their attendants were Laura, sister of the bride, and Willis Byler (Texas) and Susan Miller (Raymonds) and Bruce Troyer (Ben J.'s.)

Tablewaiters at the wedding were John Troyer (Ben B.'s) and Mary Miller (Raymonds), John Henry Miller (Raymonds) and Laura Keim (Garnett, Kansas), Marvin Zook and Marie Troyer (Townville, Pa.), David Yoder and Irene Detweiler (Marion, Ky.), Joseph H. Yoder (Becks Mills, Oh.) and Marilyn Troyer (Sugarcreek, Oh.), Aaron Hostetler

(Pa.) and Katie Shetler (Fredericksburg, Oh.), and William Yoder and Marlene Ropp (Chouteau, Ok.). Cindy Miller was helper and hostlers were David Stutzman, Steve Hochstetler and Reuben Miller. The newlyweds plan to leave today for their dairy job in Stephenville, Texas. They have bought a property here and plan to return within the next year.

Our overnight guests during and after the wedding were Vernon and Roy Coblentzes and daughters (Milroy, Ind.), Dan Coblentz, Middlebury, Ind., John Swantzes and son, Kalona, Iowa, Mrs. Floyd Bontrager and two sons, Bremen, Indiana and Milo and Amanda Miller of Nappanee, Indiana.

Amanda was telling us that her father, Levi M. Hochstetler, was a brother to John, Mart's great-grandfather. We listened with interest as she told us of the long ago days when she was a young teenager and her family was hired by John Hochstetler to work on the land he had bought in Mississippi, back then. She told of their work in the orchards and how the sky became dark one day as a cyclone hit their area. They ran for the house and all kneeled in prayer. The cyclone destroyed the packing house which stood between the two houses, but the houses remained.

Steve is helping on the carpenter crew part-time. He still can't put in a full day's work without feeling overly tired, but feels good otherwise. He enjoyed his cards and letters from young and old.

Special church services were held yesterday (Sunday, June 3) at Andy Millers' for visiting ministers. The message was brought by Bishop Ben B. Troyer of Texas and John Detweiler of Marion, Kentucky.

Ruth, five-year-old daughter of Herman Yoders, remains at the Children's Hospital in Oklahoma City. They plan to take her out of the intensive care unit today after being there a week. She is in a semiconscious state and responds some to sound and touch, but doesn't talk.

Sunday visitors at the hospital to see Ruth from this area were Herman Stutzmans and their three oldest boys and Ora Hochstetlers. This load went in the morning already. Heidi (Hermans) went up with this load. It takes about two and a half hours to make the drive. Afternoon visitors were Andy Millers, Vernon Millers, Dan Masts, and Bishop Ben B. Troyer. George Allen of Clarita took that load. A load of Herman Yoder's relatives from Haven, Kansas arrived at the hospital about noon on Sunday. Also on that load was an aunt of Herman's from Thomas, Oklahoma.

Others of this area had been to the hospital last week. Joe Masts, Herman Stutzmans and others have helped with the chores and milking. Ida's relatives from Chouteau had gone to the hospital last week. We hope to make a trip that way tomorrow or Wednesday.

A recent survey of our lease along the river shows some of the wheat and oats made it after all and the fescue field looks better than expected.

Last Tuesday morning a blazing fire destroyed ten businesses and left fourteen people homeless in downtown Coalgate. The meat and locker plant was among them. Most everyone in our community had a locker at the plant. All the meat and fruit for the wedding went up in flames just two days before it was to be served. But no one lost their lives. Cause of the fire is unknown, but arson is suspected.

June 18—Summer weather continues with temperature up to 104°. Quite a contrast from the cool and wet weather we had for so long.

Ruth Yoder came home from Oklahoma City Hospital last Monday evening. She is still gaining. She sleeps on a foam mattress on the floor so as not to fall off the bed and bump her head.

Sunday p.m. visitors at Herman Yoders' to see Ruth were Allen Yoders, Elmer Yoders, John Henry Stutzmans and the writer and son Steve. Evening callers were Raymond Millers (didn't get the names of others).

Ben J. Troyers called on John Henry Stutzmans Sunday p.m., but since they weren't home they went on to call on Winnie Patton in Clarita who is laid up with her bad foot at present.

On Saturday forenoon Steve Hochstetler, John Henry Miller and Amos A. Miller helped Vernon Miller load the hearse he restored, along with some of their belongings and some of dad's belongings. They left for Indiana via truck and trailer and plan to attend the Topeka Carriage Sale on the 20th, 21st and 22nd. The hearse is cataloged to sell at the auction. Vernon spent many hours restoring it. They will spend a week or more in Ohio, then travel to Indiana again to attend dad's wedding on the fourth. He is published to be married to Barbara Hochstetler of Topeka, Indiana. Our two boys and I plan to attend the wedding, leaving here around July 1. Vernons plan to be back by July 6 or 7. Their final move to Ohio will be in August.

Mart is still in Ohio with plans to start home Friday sometime on the bus and arrive here on Saturday.

Congratulations to *The Budget* on your 100th anniversary. We greatly enjoyed the centennial edition and want the thank the editors and staff for their efforts to supply us with this weekly paper.

Last Monday approximately 3,000 bicyclists made their way through Tishomingo, Wapanucka, and traveled along Route 48 to Route 31, then peddled eleven more miles to Coalgate where they spent the night. Their ride began in Marietta and was to end in Noel, Missouri. The trip was around 485 miles. This was the twelfth annual ride for the Free Wheel Riders. The majority were from Oklahoma, while the largest contingent of out-of-staters were from Texas. But there were participants from twenty-six states.

Melvin Hershbergers, Abe Hershberger, Mrs. Freeman Yoder and Mrs. Allen Yoder sold baked goods to the bikers from a stand and were sold out soon after lunch.

June 26—We had some much-needed rain on Sunday after several weeks of very warm weather. Some had about an inch, others one and a half inches.

Mart arrived back home Saturday night and was here to go along to church at Abe Hershbergers' Sunday. He attended the funeral of eighteen-year-old Reuben Yutzy (Aden) in West Union, Ohio on Friday before boarding the bus in Columbus for Oklahoma. Aden Yutzy and Mart were the two oldest grandsons of Grandpa Mart Hochstetlers.

At Herman Yoders' on Sunday p.m. to see Ruth were Andy Millers, Joe Masts, Dan Masts, Noah Coblentzes and us; also some young folks. Ruth has come a long ways. It's been four weeks now since the accident. She could visit some and was up a lot of the time we were there.

The ladies are busy quilting quilts for the school sale in

September. Dorothy Stutzman had one last Thursday and Anna Mary Yoder had hers at her sister Clara's today (John Henry Stutzmans).

The Raymond Miller family plans to attend the Canton, Texas flea market on Saturday and spend Sunday at Sulphur Springs, Texas. Raymonds are very busy with their crafts. Their greenhouse has closed for the season.

Area cotton fields are looking good. None of the Amish raise cotton.

There is to be a dairy meeting Wednesday evening. Seven of the families here have dairies.

The carpenters are having a busy summer schedule. Norman Miller and Robert Miller just started on Zane Breechen's new house. Yoder Construction is working on several barns and is still doing some finishing work on the large log house.

We enjoyed our company of several weeks back when we received word that one of Mart's cousins was stopping by with no clue who. So we had a nice surprise when Danny Troyer (Eli A.) and wife Nettie from Apple Creek, Ohio stepped from the van. With them were Myron Hershbergers from Texas and Myron's brother Ervin and family from Holmes County, Ohio. They brought ice cream and desserts.

———————————

July 16—We had a good rain the middle of last week which really freshened things up. The sudan grass should be ready to cut before long. Prairie hay was cut several weeks ago.

Noah and Anna Coblentz received a death message the first of the week of Mrs. Noah Miller (Fannie) of Florida.

The funeral was in Hartville, Ohio. Noahs left by bus Tuesday evening. Mrs. Ben B. Troyer from Stephenville, Texas was on the bus also. They traveled together to Missouri where they switched to car travel from there to Ohio.

Ruth Yoder (Hermans) was in church for the first time since the accident last Sunday at Melvin Hershberger's.

Two weeks ago I had mentioned that Raymond Millers had gone to Canton, Texas and then to Sulphur Springs on Sunday for church services. Elmer Yoders, Normans Millers and Robert Millers were also on the load. The Raymond Miller family went to Stephenville, Texas this weekend. Norman Millers are doing their chores and Sylvia took care of craft store customers on Saturday.

Daniel A. Hochstetlers of Clare, Michigan were visitors in the area while the boys and I were in Indiana. They were on a western trip and stopped by to visit friends and relatives. They traveled by camper. Mart was on a dozer job while they were here, but got to visit with them a little one evening.

Mart has been running a dozer for Bob Weed, making ponds for local farmers and ranchers, also clearing brush, etc. The local ranchers here call the farm ponds "tanks". Raymond Millers also had a pond made recently. Ponds are a necessity in this part of the country. Creeks dry up more quickly.

On July 13 and 14 there was a frolic at the school site to build a new schoolhouse. The shingles were all put on by Saturday p.m.

Bruce Troyer is on a trip to Kansas and Colorado with Harvey Troyers of Texas.

Malinda Miller (Andys) is still taking treatments and doing exercises to build up her muscles in the leg she had in a cast for so long, and later a brace. She isn't wearing the latter anymore.

The young folks gathered at Herman Stutzman's on Thursday for a volleyball game, and refreshments were served afterwards to remind Jacob of his twentieth birthday. He will be teaching our school again this year, being his third year teaching.

July 23—Sunny skies after three inches of rain over the weekend.

Church services yesterday at Melvin Hershbergers' for Freeman Yoders. Next services at Allen Yoders'. Visitors were Alva Yoders, Nelson Yoders and Ellen and Irene Yoder (Freeman's sisters), all of Chouteau. This load arrived Thursday. Alvas were guests at Herman Yoders'. Nelsons were at Allen Yoders' and Abe Hershbergers'. They all left Sunday evening after the singing.

Also in church were Eli and Sadie Mast of Meyersdale, Pennsylvania. They came to visit Elmer Yoders (Sadie is a sister to Elmer) and will be dinner guests at Noah Coblentzes' today. They are traveling by bus and expect to make stops in Tennessee on the way home. They made a stop here this p.m. and plan to have supper at Andy Millers', then leave Tuesday a.m.

Harvey Troyers were also in church, just arriving back from their trip to Kansas and Colorado Saturday evening. They spent the night at John Henry Stutzmans' and left for Texas Sunday p.m.

Ora Hochstetlers' guests over the weekend were also in church. They were Jonas and Betty Bontrager and daughter from Goshen, Indiana. Jonas is a cousin to Florence. They left right after church.

Herman Stutzmans and their family and Heidi Yoder arrived back from Indiana on Saturday evening. They had left Tuesday about noon with driver Ervin Raber of Kansas after receiving the shocking message that Hermans's dad, Noah Stutzman, had passed away in Florida. Funeral and burial was in Topeka, Indiana after having services in Florida first.

Hay making has come to a halt at present, so Mart will be working in the shop welding and making feeders and gates.

The grasshoppers are plentiful this year in some areas. They sit on a barbwire fence lined up beside each other, hundreds of them, as seen by passersby Sunday p.m. on the way home from church. We haven't seen many in our yard or garden yet. We have three purple martin houses around the garden which helps some.

The older purple martins are getting overanxious to have the young leave their nests so they can all be on their way south. They try and crowd the young out before they are ready. Mart put two of them up in the box again that could not fly higher than a fence post.

July 30—We have had over five inches rain since our last letter. We got caught with hay down during the rain.

The young folks took snacks and ice cream to Herman Yoders' Sunday evening to remind Heidi of her nineteenth birthday. Mart was also reminded of his birthday last week when Vernon Millers and friends of ours from Texas were here for supper one evening, bringing a cake with fifty candles.

There was a frolic at the school grounds on Saturday to work on the new schoolhouse. They put in a new waterline and put up insulation and drywall.

The big news in the community is the arrival of a baby girl named Erma at Joe and Mary Mast's. She arrived Thursday evening the twenty-sixth and has one brother and four sisters.

Robert Millers are leaving for Iowa soon to attend a family sale where Esther's grandmother's household goods, etc. will be auctioned off.

We are having an abundance of skunks in the area this summer. Some have been checked out as having rabies. So the neighborhood had the vet out to vaccinate our dogs. Mart shot two skunks today. They like to hide out in our hay barns during the day. They love to make a meal out of our baby banty chicks.

The hummingbirds are bringing their young to the feeders. We also enjoy watching the great blue heron across the road in the pond. Sometimes we also see a big white heron in the same pond. Peterson calls this big white heron a common egret. The snowy egret is smaller and has a black bill and yellow feet. The other (large white heron) has a yellow bill and black legs and feet. The cattle egrets are seen in large numbers in the pasture fields.

August 6—Sunny skies after a week of rainy weather. It finally cleared off enough to where the farmers dared cut hay. We had a very unusual wet July.

Church services were at Allen Yoder's, and to be at Raymond Miller's next time. Visiting ministers were Bishop

Ben B. Troyer of Texas and Levi Yoders of Chouteau. Levis stayed at Norman Miller's. Ray Gingerichs and Mrs. Kenneth Knepp and son were also on the Chouteau load. Rays stayed at Norman's for the night too and the Knepps were at Joe Mast's to see the new baby. Also at Joe's Sunday p.m. were Ben B. Troyer, Noah Coblentzes and us.

At Elmer Yoder's Sunday evening were John Henry Stutzmans, Vernon Millers, Ben B. Troyer and Noah Coblentzes.

We are expecting Melvin Ray Millers tomorrow. They will be unloading their belongings and Vernon Millers will be loading theirs. They expect to leave for the east early Wednesday morning with Bobby Bears as driver.

A tailless hummingbird came to the feeder today looking very unbalanced. It never did sit on the perch like the others.

Fall gardens are being planted. No irrigating necessary unless it gets dry later on.

There was a working bee at the school on Saturday. The monthly fire meeting was in Clarita this evening.

Reuben and Susan Miller left last Wednesday p.m. by bus for West Union, Ohio. Susan planned to attend a teacher's meeting in Ohio on Saturday. They plan to start back this week. Susan will be teaching school in West Union this next term.

Herman Yoders took their daughter Ruth to Oklahoma City Hospital for a checkup and scan on Friday. The doctor told them she wouldn't need to take her medicine any longer, and unless something unforeseen turns up, they don't think Ruth will need surgery, which is good news.

August 27— Our August weather has finally turned to normal with temperatures soaring up to 100° plus.

Most of the farmers have their bean hay in the barns now. It's the closest thing to alfalfa that we've baled since we left Montana five years ago. We worked in the hay field mostly in morning and evenings.

Bill Patton of Clarita goes past here about every morning back to the Boggy River to fish. He came by with a twenty-five pound catfish last week one morning. Had it in a large garbage can with water.

There was a sad incident at Olney when a fourteen-year-old local boy was lying in the middle of the road dead, last Friday night. A pickup failed to see him and drove over him, but after an autopsy, authorities said the boy had been dead for several hours. Cause of death is under investigation.

Elmer Yoders are leaving for a wedding in Missouri on Wednesday morning. They plan to be back by Friday evening.

We visited with Melvin Ray Millers on Sunday evening. They are pretty well settled in by now, and Melvin has orders for cabinets already.

A rare sight is seeing six long-legged jackrabbits going down the fencerow full speed, one behind the other. All at once the leader must have given a signal, as all six stopped at the same instant and looked around. They pounce much like a mule deer.

Some of the women are still busy quilting for the sale on September 8. The sale will be at Elmer Yoders'. Their new basement house will be finished to where it can be used by the clerks and also for quilt displays. Quite a few tents will be set up. The large barn will be used for lunch stand, bake sale and donut making.

September 4—Weather is not as humid and cooler at night, but getting dry. Lawns are turning brown.

Visitors in church at Raymond Millers' Sunday were Bishop Ben B. Troyers and Mrs. Levi Troyer (Lovina) and two children from Stephenville, Texas. From Sulphur Springs area were the Myron Hershberger family. Myron's wife Mary and daughter Tina stayed at Raymonds' overnight. They traveled on to Ohio by bus Monday. Mary Miller (Raymonds) traveled with them to Ohio to attend the wedding of James Beachy (Syl).

Labor Day visitors at Noah Coblentzes' were Bishop Andy Lapp and wife Emma and Mrs. Rachel Raber from Hartville, Ohio, Mrs. Ina Troyer from Paris, Tennessee, with drivers Lloyd and Esther Troyer of Whitevill, Tennessee. They traveled by motor home and also made stops here and at Elmer Yoders'. They were on a western trip and are on their way home now. Emma and I had traveled together about twenty-three years ago and hadn't seen each other since.

Mart is busy in the shop getting things ready for Saturday. He's welding the frames for one of the tents they will be putting up. He is also making feed troughs and hay racks to sell at the sale. We also have hay down in the bottom across the river, so it will be late to bed and early to rise this week for many in the community.

September 10—We had a welcome drizzle Friday night to lay the dust and revive the parched grass in lawns and pastures. On Saturday, September eighth, an estimated three thousand or more people arrived from all over the state and also out-of-state to attend our annual school consignment sale, which was at Elmer Yoders'. Everyone in the community put in a long day serving at lunch stand, bake sale, donut stand, pop stand, quilt consignments, parking, helping auctioneers, etc. Little boys peddled popcorn while little girls were baby-sitting.

It was the biggest turnout we've had yet with the total gross sale for merchandise being sold over the auction coming to over $60,000. The Ada Coke plant supplied us with 1,600 pounds of ice and forty-six drums of pop. They said they sold only thirty drums to the county fair. We were out of lemonade by 10:00 and served iced tea all day long as fast as we could dish it out. Donuts were sold out by 12:30. Bake sale sold out by noon and we had more baked goods this year than last year.

Top quilts were higher than ever before, but the overall average was lower than before. Top quilt went for $925, a Cameo Rose, consigned by Delores Yoder from Paris, Texas. The quilt went to Wichita Falls, Texas. Second highest was a State Flower quilt by Anna Coblentz selling for $525. This quilt went to Washington State. Quilts and wall hangings were auctioned for two hours. There were three rings going most of the time with four auctioneers present.

The people in the community began to arrive to help at five in the morning. The donut makers arrived first. The last to leave at night at 11:00 were the clerks and the ones who stayed to help the clerks.

Now Tuesday morning, the eleventh, and it's a cool, cool 62°, quite a contrast from the 90° to 100° weather we've had. Last evening the community gathered at Elmer Yoders' for a cleanup bee, taking down tents and picking up trash. The committee worked until past midnight on book work.

Coming from Garnett, Kansas for the sale were Clayton Yoder, Leander Keim, Lesley Yoder, Sarah Mae Yoder, Laura Keim and Naomi Keim. On the same load were Michael Yoder, Delbert Yoder and Harvey Yoder of Chouteau. This load stayed until Sunday evening and the young folks all got together at Herman Stutzmans' Sunday p.m. and for supper. The girls all spent Saturday night at Joe Masts'. Laura and John Troyer (Ben B.) from Stephenville, Texas also stayed until Sunday evening. Harvey Troyers and children, Sulphur Springs, stayed at John Henry Stutzmans' Saturday night and left Sunday p.m. Also here from that area were Perry Summys. The Stephenville load left Saturday evening already. On the load were Ben B. Troyers and Jonas Millers (parents to Melvin Ray Miller) and daughter Erma.

A load from Chouteau came down also for the sale with some of the women setting up a barbecue hamburger stand with proceeds going to the hospital fund for Ruth Yoder and Abe Hershbergers. A quilt and wall hanging made by this community was raffled, with proceeds also going to Ruth Yoder's hospital fund. Both were good turnouts.

We will be having church here at our place this Sunday.

September 17—A welcome rain greeted us this morning. Farmers are busy sowing wheat and rye.

Visitors at our place in church yesterday were Monroe Borntragers from northern Indiana. They arrived Friday noon and are staying at Melvin Ray Millers'. They plan to stay the most part of this week, wanting to start home Thursday or Friday, in order to get home before Sunday.

We had supper and singing here last evening with the above visitors present. Next church services at Elmer Yoders' (council meeting).

Steve left for Indiana Friday p.m. by bus. He will be staying at Leroy Millers' (his aunt Elizabeth) and wants to help Mervin Eashes with preparations for the wedding of their daughter Mary to Larry Troyer, which is on the twentieth. It is rather unusual for us to be invited to two or three weddings on the same day. Steve will be at Daniel and Erma's wedding now instead of at Mervin's. We are also invited to the wedding of Dennis Schlabach and Miriam Troyer at Jamesport, Missouri on the twentieth. We hope to start for that wedding Wednesday evening around eight and drive all night. Edwin will be going along. We plan to come back Friday.

Ida Mae Hershberger, nine-month-old daughter of Abe Hershbergers, came home from the hospital Saturday, being there since Tuesday. She had intestinal infection; the doctors were still taking some tests as to what caused it.

The young folks were going to help pick up cane at Herman Yoders' Monday evening in preparation for making sorghum Tuesday, but got rained out.

Mary Miller (Raymonds) arrived home Thursday from her trip to Ohio.

Joe Mast had attended the wedding at Eldon Kemps' at Garnett, Kansas on the sixth and came back late Friday night, just before the sale on Saturday.

The hummingbirds are getting less at the feeders. It was told we should take the feeders away now so they won't be late in their long journey south. I read an article in the paper where the people along the south Texas coast were informed to hang up feeders so the hummers could refuel before crossing the gulf.

September 24—We had five inches of rain in the past week here at the north end of the community. The Boggy River overflowed again but not as bad as in the spring. Temperature has been down since the rains, with a comfortable 80° during the day and mostly 60s or 70s during the night.

Monroe Bontragers spent the week with their daughter and family, the Melvin Ray Millers. By the time they left on Saturday there were new barn doors for the barn, the barn had a new coat of paint, and a new entrance was made and enclosed to the basement. The rain hindered some of their work, but they finished despite it.

The three of us left Wednesday evening at 8:00 with Ray Anderson as driver for Jamesport, Missouri. We drove all night and arrived in Jamesport at 5:30 Thursday morning. We ate breakfast in Jamesport and went to Bill Hostetler's to get ready for the wedding we wanted to attend at Eli Troyer's of their daughter Miriam to Dennis Schlabach (Roman) of Loganville, Wisconsin, formerly of Rexford Montana. We started back Friday forenoon and arrived home at 9:00 p.m. that evening.

Steve will be coming back from Indiana on Wednesday by bus.

The young folks gathered at Herman Stutzman's Sunday evening to remind Herman Joe of his eighteenth birthday.

Calvin Miller from Lott, Texas is taking a load to Jamesport today for the wedding of Allen Troyer (Eli) and Barbara Ann Stutzman (Atlee) which is tomorrow (Tuesday, the 25). Going from here were Raymond Millers, Ben J.

Troyers and son Bruce and John Henry Stutzmans. There are some going from Stephenville, Texas on the same load, but am not sure who.

Council meeting to be Sunday, the thirtieth, at Elmer Yoder's.

October 1—Cooler temperature over the weekend with cloudy skies, but no rain.

Farmers are still busy with fall planting of wheat and rye.

Church visitors at Elmer Yoders' yesterday were David S. Borntragers, the LaVerne Schmucker family and Minister Lester Grabers and family. Davids and LaVernes were at Andy Millers' Saturday night. Lesters spent Saturday night here with us and Sunday night at Mel Ray Millers'. Davids were at Dan Masts' Sunday night. They all wanted to visit school this forenoon and then leave from there for home in Puxico, Missouri.

Communion services to be at Norman Millers' on October fourteenth. Ben B. Troyer from Stephenville, Texas arrived at Noah Coblentzes' Saturday evening after 10:00. He plans to leave again by bus at noon today.

A load of mostly girls stopped in the community last week to visit with Mel Ray Millers and Raymond Millers. On the load were Rachel Hostetler, Anna Miller, Laura Shetler, Wayne Hostetlers, all of Fredericksburg, Ohio area and Lester Schlabach and Miriam Mullet from Goshen, Indiana. They had been on a western trip and were on their way home.

Ida Mae Hershberger (Abes) was in church again yesterday. Doctors thought cow's milk was causing the problem, so she is on soy milk now.

The load that went to Jamesport last week for the wedding of Allen Troyer and Barbara Ann Stutzman brought apples along back. We had a truck stop here in the community selling apples; there were red and golden delicious.

November 12— Allen and Freeman Yoders, Abe Hershbergers, Mrs. Ben (Esther) Troyer and Mose and Andy Hershberger came home on Friday afternoon from their eastern trip to Ohio. They also made stops in Kansas, Indiana and Tennessee visiting kinfolks.

John and Katie Ann Yoder and son William from Danville, Ohio came with the above load and are spending a few days in the area at Melvin Hershbergers'.

Melvin Hershberger had the misfortune of cutting his finger on metal on the barn roof last Thursday morning and surgery was done at Ada Hospital as the tendon was partly cut. He was in church Sunday.

Total rainfall since last Monday was one and a half inches. It is sunny and warmer again.

Persimmon trees are now about empty of their delicious fruits.

Raymond Millers, Robert Millers and Norman Millers are back from their trip to Ohio. Raymonds had a good turnout at the Ada craft show last Saturday selling and getting orders for Christmas.

Several more flocks of geese flew south last week.

Ora Hochstetler and Joe Mast were to New Mexico on a hunting trip with some good luck, bringing back some good tasting mule deer. Mart Hochstetlers are expected back this week.

It seems to get dark so early and when it does the coyotes

can be heard pretty close, as they're very plentiful.

Steve Miller (Andy) is back from his eastern trip.

November 27—Rain, rain and more rain after a week of beautiful warm and sunny weather.

Church services were at Herman Stutzmans' with a full house and quite a number of out-of-state visitors. Joe Petersheims (Dorothy's parents) of Yoder, Kansas arrived on Wednesday p.m. with Elizabeth Bontreger as driver. Hermans had been in Kansas and came along back. Joe stayed for church, then left again Monday.

Bishop Andy Stutzmans of Milroy, Indiana arrived at John Henry Stutzmans' on Thanksgiving Day. They attended church, then left Sunday p.m. by bus.

Bishop Dan Yoders of Dover, Delaware are visiting with the Andy Miller family. They arrived by bus before Thanksgiving and also attended church services.

Harvey Troyers, Mrs. Danny Joe Gingerich and two girls, Betty Marie Detweiler and the Andy Byler family, all of Texas, attended church at Hermans', too. They all left Sunday p.m.

Elizabeth Bontreger is a sister to Dan Mast of here, so she spent her time with them.

Most everyone in the community was invited somewhere for Thanksgiving dinner. At Noah Coblentzes' were Raymond Millers, Ben J. Troyers, Elmer Yoders, Dan Mast, Elizabeth Bontreger and us. At Herman Yoders' were Herman Stutzmans, Joe Petersheims, Joe Masts, Ora Hochstetlers and Melvin Ray Millers. The Melvin Hershberger family all gathered at Allen Yoders'.

Norman Millers spent Thanksgiving in Chouteau with

Sylvia's family. They stayed until Saturday, then attended the Mennonite Relief Sale at Fairview, Oklahoma. A load from Chouteau also attended, as well as a load from here. Going from our community were Elmer Yoders, Raymond Millers, Mrs. Ben J. Troyer and Freeman Yoders. Norman traveled back home with that load then.

We arrived home safely from our trip to Rexford, Montana on Wednesday morning, the fourteenth. We were busy canning venison, chili soup and stew and getting ready for our company which arrived Friday p.m. Coming from Topeka, Indiana were Ivan Jay Hochstetlers and daughter Karen, Christ Kurtz and Christina Yoder. They had attended the wedding at Cristy Millers' in Chouteau Thursday before coming here.

Levi M. Yoders, Joe Freys and their grandson had also been along on the load but stayed in Chouteau. We, along with our company, were at Melvin Ray Millers' for dinner Sunday. The young folks were all here for supper, also the Andy Miller family and Raymond Millers. Ivans left early Monday morning to pick up the rest of the load in Chouteau before going back home to Indiana.

December 3—More rain on Sunday p.m. after having some nice days last week. Last year we had a dry fall. This fall has been wet enough at the right time that the wheat and rye fields are doing good.

Last week a rather unusual rig went through the town of Coalgate. This rig was a little homemade wagon with enclosed compartments, pulled by four dogs. On the wagon was Jack Kid, a double amputee from Fredonia, Kansas. He was on his way to Houston, Texas to visit his brother. By the time he'd reached Coalgate, he'd already traveled 250 miles. Houston was still many miles down the road. He had two spare dogs tied alongside the wagon and a little puppy, which was resting contentedly on top of the wagon. What a sight!

Sunday dinner guests at Noah Coblentz's were the Melvin Hershbergers and all their married children, also Herman Stutzmans, Herman Yoders and Norman Millers.

Deer gun season lasts only a week here. The lucky ones to bring in the venison from our community were James B. Troyer and Andrew Miller.

Church to be at Joe Mast's next Sunday.

The Raymond Millers, John Henry Stutzmans and Bruce Troyers spent the weekend in Texas. They were at the flea market in Canton on Saturday and spent Sunday in Sulphur Springs area.

1991 Coalgate, Oklahoma

March 11—Temperature was in the 80s last week, but turned cooler over the weekend and very windy. It's getting on the dry side.

Had lots of visitors in the community over the weekend. At Ben B. Troyers' and Noah Coblentzes' were Noah Byler, James Bylers, Melvin B. Troyers, and John Millers, all of Pennsylvania. The Bylers were from Harrisville and the others from Smicksburg. John and wife Barbara had supper with us Sunday evening and stayed overnight. Barbara was a Troyer and is a cousin to my dad. Had never met her before. That load was all at Elmer Yoders' for Sunday dinner and left early Monday morning before the rooster crowed.

At Herman Stutzmans' were Joe Petersheim Srs., Joe

and Edna Petersheim and five children of Yoder, Kansas. They came Saturday morning and left Sunday p.m. Joe and Edna and children were at Ora Hochstetlers', too. Their driver was Ervin Raber. His wife Naomi and son Joseph were along.

At Joe Masts' were Danny Joe Gingerichs and two girls, Willis Bontragers and Betty Marie Detweiler from Sulphur Springs, Texas. Bobby Bear was their driver. Also along on that load was Darrel Troyer of Sulphur Springs (Como) and Junior Kauffman from Rexford, Montana. They were here for Sunday dinner and went along to the young folks' gathering at Dan Masts' with our boys.

At Dan Masts' were Miriam and Robert Gingerich (Andy) and Naomi Gingerich (Joe) from Texas. The two girls stayed until Monday p.m. then left by bus. The rest of the Texas load left Sunday evening.

Junior Kauffman went along back to Texas and plans to leave from there for Indiana this week unless he finds a job for several months which suits him.

Melvin Ray Millers were at Norman Millers' Sunday p.m. Herman Yoders spent Sunday p.m. at Herman Stutzmans' and Ora Hochstetlers spent the day at Hermans'. Norman Millers were here Sunday evening. They and John and Barbara Miller have both gone through the same experience. Johns also lost a seven-year-old daughter while on her way to school. She was walking when struck by a car. This happened many years ago. This was their oldest daughter but not an only child.

The purple martin scouts were here several days ago.

Noah Coblentzes and Mrs. Ben B. Troyer are leaving by bus late tonight to attend a wedding in St. Mary's, Ontario.

Andy Millers and daughter Kathryn and son Andrew are leaving this evening by bus to attend the wedding of a niece and cousin in Pennsylvania and want to visit other relatives in the east before returning home.

Daniel Troyer (Ben B.) and son are here at Bens'. They arrived Sunday p.m. from Jamesport, Missouri.

March 18—We're having genuine spring weather.

We were asked to write until the Hochstetlers come back from their trip to Ohio for a wedding this week, leaving Monday morning. The boys stayed at home to do chores.

We saw purple martins at our martin house last week but not since. It was getting rather dry here but were blessed with a nice shower Saturday evening. By Sunday morning we had a total of 2.4 inches. Pasture land is already greening up and gave the gardens a boost, too. Our strawberry plants are still blooming. It was getting dry enough that we were watering them and the garden.

There was a birthday surprise last Thursday evening at Melvin Hershbergers' for son Mose with the young folks attending, then when some of them were on the way home Herman Stutzman's horse kicked up some kind of paper and if flew up behind their buggy scaring the horse behind them which was Raymond Millers' young folks and the three passengers were dumped into the ditch, also breaking the shafts. They hitched a ride home with Hermans' young folks along with the horse, then used Hermans' buggy to go on home. Reuben wasn't in church Sunday on account of a sore knee and is on crutches.

Some of you might know Floyd Nelson. He had back surgery March sixth. Joe Masts and Herman Stutzmans went to visit him Thursday evening. He seems to be doing real well.

Noah Coblentzes and Mrs. Emma Troyer plan on being home this week sometime from their trip north.

Daniel Troyer and son James were visiting at Bens' last week. After having a bit of a hassle with bus connections they finally left Friday.

The Amish school consignment committee got together last week at Raymond Millers' to make plans for this year's sale.

Church was at Herman Yoders' and had council meeting. Next services at Raymond Millers', communion services.

September 16—A cool 72° and raining. Looks like we might get several inches, or close to it. The weather was very appreciated on Saturday with clouds to hide the sun most of the day. Just after the sale was all over it poured for awhile. Some were caught in it on the way home.

The school sale is over for another year. An estimated 5,000 people gathered to take part in the event with cars parked all the way to Jct. 31 and in Norman Miller's field, plus the usual parking at Elmer Yoder's where the sale took place. Everyone had their hands full with the job assigned to them. We appreciated the extra help when Chouteau people offered their help. There were at least three loads here from Chouteau. They also had a hamburger stand and bake sale separate from ours to help raise funds for some of their large hospital bills. Our school funds should be supplied for another year.

The quilts brought good prices with the highest one

bringing $2,000, a peach and green morning glory appli-
que by Sylvia Miller. Runner-up was a blue, mauve, and
peach Country Bride applique by Mrs. Allen (Mary) Yoder. Three quilts brought $1,000.

The overall prices for most quilts were much higher than
last year. We had sixty-one cataloged quilts, plus fifteen to
twenty others.

The highest horse brought $1,150, a registered Morgan
stallion. Quite a few of the exotic animals that were con-
signed didn't show up for the sale, but the fowl and dogs
brought good prices.

Church services were at Dan Masts' Sunday with a lot
of out-of-state visitors present. From Ohio were Emanuel
D. Miller, Ben J. Rabers and Andy Rabers. They arrived
Friday p.m. and left Monday a.m. They lodged at Norman
Millers' and Raymond Millers' and lended helping hands
at the sale. At Noah Coblentzes' was the Levi Mast family,
formerly of Sarasota. They moved to Ohio now. They arrived Thursday and left after the sale.

From Bonduel, Wisconsin were Mel Troyers (Harvey's
parents) and LaVern Troyers (Harvey's brother) and
daughter (Spencer). They traveled by train and were going on to Oregon. From Garnett, Kansas were Ira Yoders and son Ray (Wilma's parents and brother), and from
LaRussell, Missouri were Herman Schrocks (Harvey's sister). These all lodged at Harveys'. Also from Garnett were
Johnny Yoders who were at Herman Yoders'. These were
all at the sale, too.

On the Stephenville, Texas load were Edwin Millers, Levi
B. Troyers and children, Jonas Millers and Matthew, and
Joe Gingerich. Edwin Millers and Mrs. Levi Troyer (Lovi-

na) and children are staying at their parents', the Raymond Millers, since Edwin has off one week. Jonas Millers, Levi Troyer and Joe Gingerich left Sunday p.m. after church. Their driver was Calvin Miller and family from Lott, Texas.

Those that came just for the sale were Joe Petersheims Sr., who were at Herman Stutzmans', and Sam Bontragers who had a harness booth at the sale. Both were from Haven, Kansas. Sams spent the night with us.

Ben J. Troyer and wife Esther and son James just came back from Ohio last night after attending Ben's mother's funeral and Esther's niece's wedding. Esther had been in Ohio for quite awhile.

May 20—Another half inch of rain Sunday evening. A lot of hay down. Gardens are doing well this year.

Noah and Anna Coblentz and Melvin Ray Millers arrived back Sunday evening. The driver took Jonas Millers and daughter Emma and Matthew on home yet to Stephenville, Texas.

Reuben and Willis Byler from Stephenville were at Ben B. Troyer's over the weekend. They plan on moving to Fredericksburg, Ohio area in the near future.

Raymond Millers and Norman Millers arrived back Thursday evening from their trip to Ohio.

Perry Summys of Sulphur Springs area were here in the area last week on business. They bought the Everett Kreb's property across the road from us (ten acres). They plan to move a trailer in soon. Harvey Troyers plan to move into Perry's trailer the first Monday in June until their building is ready to move into. Perry's ten acres joins Harvey's place.

Yoder Construction finished their job in Abilene, Texas on Friday and plan to start on Harvey's large shop today. Norman Miller had been helping Darrel with the cement work.

This will be my last week for baking. I baked Thursdays and Fridays and took it to town to sell on Saturdays. Heidi Yoder (Herman) helped me one or two days a week. Since school is out one of her younger sisters has come along to wash dishes.

Elmer Yoders are having company from Ontario, Canada over the weekend. These two families were former employees of Yoders.

Part II

Schools, Families and Homesteads

IN PART II OF THIS BOOK WE WANT TO INTRODUCE you to the families of the Clarita Amish settlement. We begin with a look into our annual school auction then move to a personal glimpse of each family with pictures of each of their homesteads.

We hope it is accurate enough to give an idea what the Clarita settlement in Oklahoma was like. It is still thriving today.

We've heard Oklahoma being described as "tornado alley" or "the land of extremes".

We do know that the weather can be very wet or extremely warm and dry. But other places in the country have the same.

The families who have lived there for a long time now have tried to adapt accordingly and find it possible to live in that weather zone.

A few of the families have shared their aerial views of their farms, thus giving a more clear picture of the lay of the land.

We do want to thank them for this, and also thanks to all for the information and cooperation when we were out to take notes.

Special thanks to Maxine Groves for taking me to Oklahoma and for taking photos of the farms and properties.

As mentioned before, most or all of the Clarita Amish had Route 5 Coalgate for their mailing address. Coalgate is Coal County's main town or county seat.

May we give all the honor and praise to our almighty God in Heaven.

chapter eight

Clarita Amish Schools

Year	Name	Teacher	Teacher's Address	No. of Pupils
1980-81	Hardwood	Lena Mast	Coalgate, OK	14
1980-81	Ash Flat	Ada Hershberger	Coalgate, OK	15
1981-82	Elm Creek	Mrs. Nettie Beiler	Coalgate, OK	11
1981-82	Lone Star	Ada Hershberger	Coalgate, OK	9
1982-83	Lone Star	Mary Hershberger	Coalgate, OK	10
1983-84	Lone Star	Mary Hershberger	Coalgate, OK	14
1984-85	Lone Star	Mary Hershberger	Coalgate, OK	18
1985-86	Lone Star	Mary Hershberger	Coalgate, OK	16
1986-87	Elm Creek	Edward Yoder	Bloomfield, IA	14
1987-88	Elm Creek	Edward Yoder	Coalgate, OK	12
1988-89	Elm Creek	Jacob Stutzman	Coalgate, OK	18
1989-90	Elm Creek	Jacob Stutzman	Coalgate, OK	14
1990-91	Elm Creek	Jacob Stutzman	Coalgate, OK	16
1991-92	Elm Creek	Jacob Stutzman	Coalgate, OK	23

1992-93	Elm Creek	Jacob Stutzman	Coalgate, OK	24
1993-94	Elm Creek	Nathan Schrock	Haven, KS	27
		Mrs. Alma Summy	Coalgate, OK	
1994-95	Elm Creek	Miriam Stutzman	Coalgate, OK	29
		Mrs. Alma Summy	Coalgate, OK	
1995-96	Elm Creek	Katie Keim	Garnett, KS	20
		Mrs. Ada Yoder	Coalgate, OK	
		Carol Mast	Coalgate, OK	
1996-97	Elm Creek	Miriam Stutzman	Coalgate, OK	21
		Mrs. Ada Yoder	Coalgate, OK	
1997-98	Elm Creek	Miriam Stutzman	Coalgate, OK	22
		Mrs. Ada Yoder	Coalgate, OK	
1998-99	Elm Creek	Miriam Stutzman	Coalgate, OK	23
		Mrs. Ada Yoder	Coalgate, OK	
1999-00	Elm Creek	Miriam Stutzman	Coalgate, OK	20
		Mrs. Ada Yoder	Coalgate, OK	
2000-01	Elm Creek	Miriam Stutzman	Coalgate, OK	21
		Elsie Yoder	Coalgate, OK	
2001-02	Elm Creek	Elsie Yoder	Coalgate, OK	19
		Ada Yoder	Coalgate, OK	
2002-03	Elm Creek	Elsie Yoder	Coalgate, OK	19
		Elizabeth Yoder	Coalgate, OK	

Elm Creek School is still in use today with 19 pupils for the 2002-2003 term.

This is Lone Star schoolhouse in Melvin Hershbergers' back yard. It is no longer in use.

Clarita Amish School Consignment Auction

I N 1988, THE 24TH OF SEPTEMBER, VERNON E.
Millers had the first annual school consignment sale.
They had it in the second year too. Then Elmer Yoders took
the annual auction for five years. After that the auction has
been at Ben B. Troyers for the last eight years. The last auction in September 2002, being the fifteenth year.

By the fifth year the crowd had blossomed to five thousand or over. By 1996 they were expecting from ten to fifteen thousand. Today there's an estimated fifteen to twenty
thousand people showing up for the big day. Cars are parked
all over the 278 acre farm plus the neighbor's fields too.

The auction has become one of the most anticipated
events in the state, with people coming from Texas, California, Washington, and many other states too. And even
Australia! There are lots of craft and antique booths where a
lot of non-Amish will have their arts and crafts on sale. It's
like a flea market plus an auction.

The quilts (over one hundred) are always a big attraction.
There are many wall hangings too. The job of parking cars
takes twenty to thirty people. A church group (non-Amish)
handles the parking. They charge $1.00 per car and use the
money as a fundraiser for their church. Sometimes parking
goes to other local charities and the local fire department.

Pancakes and sausage are served from 6:00 in the morning until 10:00 a.m. There are lunch stands and bake sales,
with the proceeds plus all commissions going to Clarita

Amish School. There are horses to sell, plus saddles, tack, sheep, goats, and fowl. There's farm equipment, tractors, horse and cattle trailers. If you care for antiques, there are collectibles, guns, glassware, linens, crafts, furniture of all descriptions—inside and outside. There is a large assortment of merchandise; there are items of interest to everyone. There's lots of food for everyone. People usually come early and stay late. There are from three to four auctioneers selling at the same time in different areas. Morris Yoder of Millersburg, Ohio helped auction off the quilts since 1997. By the end of the auction, the Clarita Amish men and women, boys and girls and all who come from out of state or other areas to help, are bone weary, but thankful to have enough money for their school for another year.

There is a lot of baking involved the day before the sale. The Clarita Amish ladies bake and bake and bake some more. They have no Amish bakery nearby to bake their quotas for them. Each one gets a slip on what and how much to bake.

1st Annual
Amish School Consignment
AUCTION
September 24th—10:00 A.M.
Quilts sell at 1:00 P.M.

LOCATED at CLARITA CARRIAGE One mile east of Hwy 48, between Tupelo and Clarita, 35 miles North of Durant or 35 miles southeast of Ada, Ok and 11 miles west of Coalgate

QUILTS
1 Pieced Sampler, 1 Quilted Sampler, 2 Granmothers Fans, 1 Candlewicking Sampler, 1 Amish Diamond, 1 Log Cabin, 1 Humming bird, 1 Peach\Blue Plain Top, 1 Peach\Beige Plain Top, 1 Flower Basket, 1 Patchwork Quilt, 1 Knotted Quilt, 1 Kings X Crib Quilt, 1 Variable Star Crib Quilt, 2 Unbleached Muslin Crib Quilts, 100 Yr. Old Plain Quilt, Old Flower Basket

WALLHANGINGS
1 Pinwheel, 1 Lonestar, 1 Dahlia, 1 Variable Star, 1 Granmothers Fan, 2 Mapleleaf, 1 rocking Horse, 1 Amish girl, 1 Hearts, 2 Horses, 1 Hummingbird

HOUSEHOLD ITEMS
2 Treadle Tables, 2 Lavatories, 2 Countertop Sinks, 1 Cupboard w\glass Doors, Babycrib, Recliner, Couch, 2 Baby Strollers & Seats, 3 Wringer Washer, Quilt Frame, 2 Gas Lanterns, 2 Kerosene Lamps, Produce Scale, 2 Typewriters, Propane Heaters, Metal Kitchen Sink, Top Cabinets, Gas Cookstove, Misc. Kitchen & Glassware, Bunkbeds, Swivel Desk Chair, Bed Frame w/Head and ft. boards, Glass Jars, Aluminum Stormwindows

HORSE DRAWN VEHICLES & IMPLEMENTS
Cozy Cab Buggy, Breaking Cart, Open Buggy, Buggy W/Top, Rubber Tire Pony Wagon, 3 Seat Pony Surrey, Steel Wheeled Wagon, 2 Hay Wagons, Sleigh, Road Cart, 2 Horse, Walking Cultivator, Walking Plow, 1 Row Planter, Grain Binder, Case Roller Bar Hayrake, International Hay Mower, Double Shovel Plow, Disc.

HORSES & HARNESSES
1 Morgan Yearling gelding, 2 Yearling Belgian, Quarter Horse Cross, 2 Smooth Mouth Ponies Broke to Ride & Drive-Kid Safe, Saddlebred Colt, Halter, Broke, Weanling, 1 Saddlebred-Morgan Colts Halter Broke, Weanling, 4 yr. old Standardbred gelding, Broke to Drive, 11 yr. old Standardbred Mare, Broke to Drive, Used Leather Buggy Harness #3 Sets, Nylon Work Harness w/ Collars, Hames With Tugs, Harness Parts, Work Harness

FARM & MISCELLANEOUS
Air Compressors, 30 gal. portable, 100 Gallon Airtank, 250 Gallon Propane Tank, Ornamental Buggy Wheels, 3 Martin Houses, 2 Wheeled Dolly, 2 Saddles, Reel Push mower,

Bandsaw, Wisconsin Motor 2 Cyl. 12 H.P., 2 Wisconsin Engines 1 good for Parts, Tractor, Fordson Major 5000, Miller Roughneck Welder (As is), 1975 Chevy Pickup, 14 ft. Stock Trailer, Corral Panels 10, 12, 14, & 16 ft., 4 Wheeled Wagon, 2 Round Hog Self Feeders, New Metal Storage Building, 8 x 12, Wheel Barrow, Water Pump, Pump Hose unit for Septic cleaning system, 1 air compressor, 10 H.P., Industrial size

ANTIQUES & COLLECTIBLES
Hand Wool Carding Machine, Blue Jars with Glass Lids, Hand Cranked Washer, Amish Dolls, Handwoven Rugs, 12 Gauge Magnum Remington Automatic, Oak Table with Matching Buffet (and 6 cane chairs), Treadle Sewing Machine, Table with 2 leaves, bed & dresser, cream can, Turtle Footstools, Horse hide buggy robe

FARM ANIMALS & FOWL
Ducks, Rabbits, 2 Bull Calves- Holstein, 2 Butcher Hogs, 3 Open Gilts-Mkt. wt., 100 Laying pullets, 12 Laying hen, 5 pr. Bantys, 2 roosters, 2-6 month old treeing Walker pups, Purple Ribbon Breed

The Amish Ladies will have a Lunch Stand and Bake Sale—Lots of Home Baked Goodies

We will be taking Consignments up to day of sale. Let us sell your merchandise.
COMMISSION SCHEDULE— 4% on items over $500, 8% on items $250 to $500, 12% on items up to $250. Half Commision on P.O. items. NO JUNK PLEASE.

TO CONSIGN or FOR MORE INFORMATION CONTACT

Vernon Miller
R. 5 Coalgate
Ok. 74538

OR

Call
Andy Miller
405-428-3220

Lunch Stand and Bake Sale and all Commissions go for Clarita Amish School

Winnwoods Country Furniture and Millers Country Crafts will have Booths of their Crafts and Tole Painting

Auctioneers:
Chillie Joe Bills
Fred Shivers
Don Lawrence

Not Resposible for Accidents

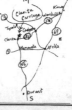

2002 AUCTION

Quilts	93,686.00
Antiques	30,472.50
Buggies, Machinery and tack	7,243.40
Poultry and other livestock	493.43
Horses	4,578.50

CLARITA LUNCH STAND

Gross sale	9,505.00
Expenses	2,527.34
Profit	6,977.66

POP STAND

Gross sales	5,997.65
Expenses	2,123.90
Profit	3,873.75

BAKE SALE

Gross sales	23,378.65
Paid out to consigners	20,038.65
Sub total	3,339.83
Tent	384.00
Profit	2,955.83

LUNCH STAND AND BAKE SALE
@ 10% commission

Kansas sales	564.00
Chouteau sales	2,984.86
D. Knepp	(included in booth commission)
Profit	3,548.86

BOOTHS

Booths	11,920.00
Booth commission @ 10%	908.00
Sub total	12,828.00
Tents	3,984.00
Booth applications and postage	92.34
Profit	8,751.66

Parking

Clarita Fire Department	446.30
R.V. Parking	210.00

BALANCE IN BANK

July 1, 2002	21,705.92
November 1, 2002	38,657.21

School auction financial report.

2002 QUILTS

FULL SIZE QUILTS		AVERAGE	GROSS SALES	COMMISSION
Coalgate	67	$899	$60,250	$9,037.50
Chouteau	11	527	6,250	937.50
Missouri	2	1,212	2,425	363.75
Kansas	4	556	2,225	333.75
Boley	8	506	4,050	607.50
Ohio	5	545	2,725	408.75
Canada	12	712	8,550	1,282.50
totals	109	all 793	$86,475	$12,971.25

WALL HANGERS - CRIB - COMFORTERS

Coalgate	37	$4,110	$616.50
Chouteau	1	225	33.75
Missouri	1	100	15.00
Kansas	1	55	8.25
Boley	8	1,315	197.25
Ohio	1	85	12.75
Canada	2	240	36.00
totals	51	$6,130	$919.50

OTHER	carpets-baskets-flowers	$1,081	$162.15
	TOTALS	$93,686	$14,052.90

EXPENSES

Tent	$740.00		
Morris Yoder @ 7%	$6,556.62		
Saftey pins	4.21	COMMISSION	$14,052.90
total	$7,300.83	EXPENSES	7,300.83
		TOTAL PROFIT	$6,752.07

QUILT RAFFLE   Starlight Compass

Tickets sold	$2.393.50	
Quilt expense	173.20	
Tablets	6.33	
profit	$2,215.91	$2,215.91

Winner - Lisa Troyer, Jamesport, MO

QUILT BOOKS SOLD

	$266.00	
Printing	174.62	
profit	91.77	$91.77
	GRAND TOTAL PROFIT	$9,059.75

Highest quilt $3,000

School auction financial report.

12th Annual
Clarita
AMISH SCHOOL
CONSIGNMENT
AUCTION
and Lots of Craft-Antique Booths
to browse through on sale day.

SEPTEMBER						
S	M	T	W	T	F	S
			1	2	3	4
5	6	7	8	9	10	11
12	13	14	15	16	17	18
19	20	21	22	23	24	25
26	27	28	29	30		

Saturday, September 11th, 1999 - 8:30 a.m.

LOCATION: Clarita, OK - Ben Troyer Farm, Hwy. 48 - between Tupelo & Clarita. 35 miles north of Durant, 35 miles SE of Ada, 11 miles west of Coalgate, 1/2 mile east of former site. (see map on back)

NOTICE
MasterCard & Visa Only Accepted

More Than 100 Beautiful Hand Quilted Quilts,
Plus Many Wall Hangings, etc.

FARM EQUIP. & MOTOR VEHICLES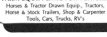
Horses & Tractor Drawn Equip., Tractors,
Horse & Stock Trailers, Shop & Carpenter
Tools, Cars, Trucks, RV's

ANTIQUES
Collectibles, Guns, Glassware, Linens, Crafts,
Handcrafted and Antique Furniture, etc.

 BUGGIES & WAGONS
Harness, Saddles, Tack, etc.
Sheep, Goats, Poultry, etc.

CRAFT - ANTIQUE BOOTH & SALE
The Amish Ladies Will Have A Lunch Stand & Bake Sale.
Lots Of Home Baked Goodies & Whole Hog Sausage.

Come Early and Enjoy Donuts and Coffee (Pancakes and Sausage served from 6:00 to 10 a.m.)

Lunch Stand, Bake Sale & All Commissions go to Clarita Amish School

Parking

$10.00 Bus Parking and $1.00 Per Car
Benefits Local Charities

Consignments

The general public is invited to consign items to be auctioned off.
Contact (580) 428-3421, 428-3014 or 428-3114

MORRIS
YODER
AUCTIONEER
330-674-6623
OHIO

AUCTIONEERS

E. J. Chupp
918-543-2746

Al McKay
580-622-2612

TERMS: Cash, approved check or credit cards day of sale. We hold registration papers on horses & titles on motor vehicles, when paid by check until check clears. If you purchased large items that you cannot move on the sale date, you may pick them up later by showing your ticket. However, you leave articles at your own risk, neither seller, land owner nor Auction Co. assumes responsibility for any item. We do not work on Sunday so items must be removed by sale date or Monday thru Saturday thereafter. Items not removed within 15 days become property of sale committee. Oklahoma law requires collecting sales tax unless proof of sales tax exemption is furnished.

CONSIGNMENT INFORMATION: All consignments welcome except Quilts. Quilts sold at Auction are quilted by Amish & Mennonite ladies only. Consignments will be taken until 9:00 a.m. day of Sale.

COMMISSION SCHEDULE: Livestock 10%, all other items 20% per item up to $250.00. 10% per item over $250.00. P.O. Charge 10% or not to exceed $25.00. A minimum of $1.00 commission per ticket.

Booth Information (580) 428-3463
Quilt Information (580) 428-3458

Partial List of Consignments

Horses, buggies, harness, collars, etc.
1900's Furniture, oak dresser, oak drop leaf table, mahogany tables, washstand , glassware etc.
Our antique auction gets better every year!

Please Patronize the following Businesses Who Have Sponsored this Brochure

Hefty Trashbags and Kraft Cereals
Diapers-Huggies
Home & Garden Products

John & Kathy Troyer

 Troyers Groc. Outlet

Campbells & Progresso Soups
Laundry Soaps-Household Cleaners

Open 8:30 - 5:00 Mon - Sat
Closed Sundays and Wednesday
Located at Auction Site

Route 5 Box 410
Coalgate, Oklahoma 74538
(580) 428-3021

 **Miller Crafts**

CUSTOM WOODCRAFT &
DECORATIVE TOLE PAINTING

Raymond & Elsie Miller

(580) 428-3463
Route 5, Box 1365 • Coalgate, Oklahoma 74538

 **GREENHOUSE**

GARDENING AS FINE ART
1708 S. W. 24th •• Norman, OK 73072
Tel 405-321-3744
NANCY STAGGS JARMON

 **Kountry Store**
In Tupelo, OK
FULL SERVICE STORE

• GAS
• GROCERIES

• ICE
• FISHING SUPPLIES

845-2652

Dollar Bills

Gas   Deli
Grocery   Ice
All You Can Eat Buffet!
Corner of 7 and 48   Wapanucka

 FNB

MEMBER
FDIC

MAY WE HELP YOU?

Phone 580-927-2311   Fax 580-927-2153
Coalgate, Oklahoma
www.shamrockbank.com

Plantation
SUITES

1909 Highway • Port Aransas, Texas 78373
Local 361-749-3866
Toll-Free 1-877-836-3866
www.plantationsuites.com

NOTES:

✗ Sale conducted rain or shine.
✗ Many Large Tents & Barns on Premises
✗ Limited Rough Camping Spots Available at $20 (no hookups)

AUCTION SCHEDULE:

Antiques, Furniture, household items - begin 8:30 a.m.
Farm equipment, motor vehicles - begin 10:00 a.m.
Antique Furniture - begins 11:00 a.m.
Quilts - begin 12:30 p.m.
Livestock - begin 11:30 - 12:00 p.m.

In order to get everything sold in the alloted time period, it will be necessary to conduct 3 or more auction rings at the same time. Any announcements day of sale supercedes all other announcements or advertising.

AUCTIONEER'S NOTE: You will want to plan to spend the entire day at this huge auction that grows larger each year. Estimated attendance last year was between 15,000 and 20,000 people. With such a large assortment of merchandise, there are bargains and items of interest to everyone. Much of the time there may be 3 and 4 auctioneers selling at the same time in different areas.

Since most consignments are not known until closer to sale date, it is impossible to list the items individually at time of this printing. This will be the only flyer prior to the auction.

Come early, stay late and be prepared to enjoy the auction, the variety of booths, the wonderful food and fellowship.

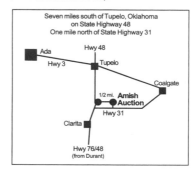

Seven miles south of Tupelo, Oklahoma
on State Highway 48
One mile north of State Highway 31

Clarita School Consignment Auction
Rt. 5, Box 450
Coalgate, OK 74538

The sign at the end of Elmer Yoders' driveway on auction day, 1991.

1991. parking on either side of the road in Elmers' field and Normans' field. Andy Millers' house in the background.

More parking in Harveys' and Normans' fields. Harveys' place in the background. This was in 1991 and the last sale Marts attended before moving the first of December.

Buggy parking on auction day.

Harness and tack all in a row.

This is at Vernon Millers, the second year of the auction at Clarita Carriage in 1989.

chapter nine

Families and Homesteads

1. Raymond E. Millers
2. Ben J. Troyers
3. Crist J.C. Yoders
4. Melvin J. Troyers
5. Norman E. Millers
6. Daniel C. Masts
7. Melvin J. Hershbergers
8. Ben W. Hostetlers
9. Menno E. Yoders
10. John B. Beachys
11. Ben B. Troyers
12. Noah J. Coblentzs
13. Andrew Beilers
14. Lonnie Millers
15. Willie Millers
16. Atlee Stutzmans
17. Vernon E. Millers
18. Melvin Ray Millers
19. Herman R. Yoders
20. Elmer Yoder, Jrs.
21. John Henry Stutzmans
22. Herman Stutzmans
23. Andy A. Miller, Jrs.
24. Martin Hochstetlers
24-A. Elmer Troyers
25. Allen Yoders
26. Abe Hershbergers
27. Edward Yoders
28. Freeman Yoders
29. Cristie Millers
30. Ora J. Hochstetlers
31. Joe L. Masts
32. Robert Millers
33. Harvey M. Troyers
34. Perry Summys
35. Joseph J. Petersheims
36. Jonas L. Millers
37. David Stutzmans
38. Andrew Millers
39. David Lee Yoders
40. Edwin Millers
41. Levi Troyers
42. Jacob Stutzmans
43. John Henry Millers
44. Ervin J. Yoders
45. Reuben Millers
46. Herman Joe Stutzmans
47. Daniel Troyers
48. John Troyers
49. David H. Yoders
50. Nathan Stutzmans

There were actually 52 families, but we have Elmer Troyers as 24-A and Joe Schmuckers are not numbered. They lived in Coleman but came to Clarita for church.

CLARITA AMISH CHURCH
BISHOP Ben B. Troyer

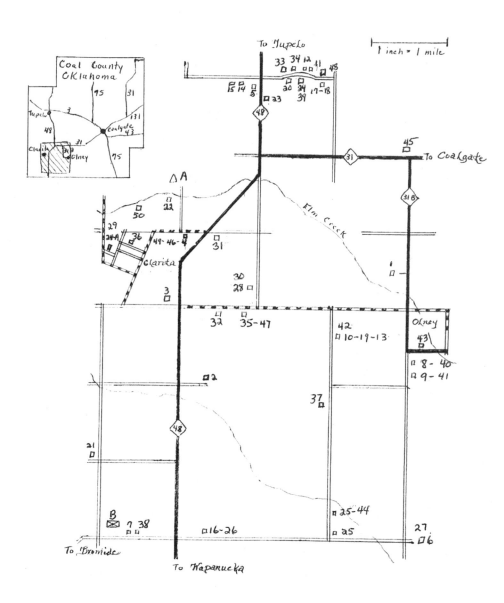

Family #1—Raymond & Elsie Miller

In the spring of 1978 several Amish men from the Sugar-creek, Ohio area decided to take a trip to Coal County, Oklahoma, to check out some land that was advertised in *The Budget* by a real estate company from Oklahoma.

It was the time of year when the farmers were plowing the rich soils in the hills of Holmes and Tuscarawas Counties, and getting ready for their spring planting.

Raymond Miller, Ben J. Troyer, Sylvanus H. Beachy, (brother-in-law to Raymond), and Amos Yoder left the hills behind and headed for the prairie grasslands of Oklahoma, where the local and rural farmers were raising cotton and hay grazer. This marked the beginning of the Clarita Amish settlement.

In May of 1978 another trip was made when Raymond

Raymond and Elsie Miller's house.

Raymonds' craft shop where the wedding dinners were served for their daughters' weddings. The back of the craft shop is now used for their whelping house. No more crafts. The dogs took over.

and Elsie attended a wedding in Jamesport, Missouri, then met Ben J. and Esther Troyer in St. Louis coming out to Oklahoma to shop for land. Also along on the load were three of Raymond's sisters and husbands, Ben and Emma Raber, Delbert R. and Elizabeth Troyer, and Emanuel D. and Mabel Miller.

The Oklahoma land was cheaper than the rising prices of land and farms in Holmes County and surrounding areas. By fall of that same year the Millers were moving on a farm near Clarita, Oklahoma.

Raymond E. Miller was born March 16, 1942. He was the son of Noah N. and Lovina (Yoder) Miller of Sugarcreek, Ohio-RRI. He married October 31, 1963, to Elsie B. Hostetler, born May 30, 1943, daughter of Benj. W. and

Alma (Beachy) Hostetler of Sugarcreek, Ohio, RRI. Raymond was ordained minister May 17, 1968.

On October 23, 1978, they loaded up their belongings and with the help of neighbors, friends, and relatives they moved to their new home in Coal County, Oklahoma. The first Amish church service was held at Raymonds on November 19, 1978.

Children of Raymond and Elsie

#32. Robert	September 17, 1964
#40. Edwin	November 22, 1965
Susan	August 16, 1967

Susan married Robert (Roys) Raber on September 17, 1993 and moved to West Union, Ohio.

#41. Lovina	October 2, 1968
Mary	December 25, 1969

Mary married Marlin (Pauls) Beachy on May 7, 1999 and moved to Trail, Ohio (Dundee).

#43. John Henry	March 16, 1972
#45 Reuben	November 1, 1973
Willis	February 8, 1975 - Stillborn
#46. Lucinda (Cindy)	August 8, 1976

Raymonds raised calves until they had their dairy herd and started milking. Robert was fourteen years old when they moved and was out of school. Edwin was in the eighth grade. Both boys helped their neighbors and local farmers haul hay in the evenings.

The children went to Olney public school until they had their own school for the Amish community.

On August 30, 1983, Raymonds moved to (Route 1, Box 14CC) Stephenville, Texas with their family to work on a large dairy. They moved back to the Clarita settlement again June 30, 1988, this time to a place closer to Olney. Here they had a wood shop and made crafts to sell. Elsie painted a lot of their woodcrafts and helped a lot with other projects too.

By this time Robert and Lovina had already married and stayed in Texas to continue working on dairies for awhile. Susan worked out some after Raymonds came back from Texas until she went to teach school in West Union, Ohio where she met her future husband, Robert Raber.

At the time of this writing Raymond and Elsie are still living in the Clarita settlement near Olney. Their children are all married and have homes of their own. Raymonds have put up dog kennels and are raising puppies to sell, which seems like a promising business at this time. A broker comes

One of the outside dog kennels at Raymonds.

Another dog kennel at Raymonds which helps keep Raymond busy.

around every week to pick up what puppies are ready.

They no more make and sell crafts. They are kept busy raising dogs. They have the whelping house (nursery) in the back part of the craft shop. Elsie takes care of that. They raise Yorkies, Minipins, Schüzu Havenese, Cocker Spaniels, Eskimos, Dockson, and more. Raymond takes care of the kennels outside. He also has some fowl he raises and spends some time in their perennial flower beds.

Elsie has a nice garden with raised beds and keeps the garden and housework in order between her whelping house chores. She also quilts for the annual school auction.

Asian pear trees bloom along the drive in the spring and beautiful redbuds make a striking color scene against the blue Oklahoma sky.

Raymond is an uncle to Norman, #5, and Vernon, #17. Elsie is a sister to Irene, #9, and a daughter to Ben and Alma

Hostetler, #8.

Family #2—Ben & Esther Troyer

On November 14, 1978, about three weeks after the Raymond Miller family moved to Oklahoma, Ben and Esther Troyer and their two sons, Bruce and James, moved to Coalgate Route 5.

Despite the heat from the summer sun and the wide cracks in the ground from lack of moisture, the four families, Minister Raymond Millers, Minister Ben J. Troyers, Minister Crist J.C. Yoders, and Melvin J. Troyers felt led by the Lord to buy land in Oklahoma that summer of 1978. Now it was time to make the move.

Bruce was thirteen years old and James was six. Bens and Crists (family #3) both moved in the same week, only a day apart.

Ben J. and Esther Troyer's house.

The shop and buggy shed at Bens' place.

There was a lot of work to do on the farm Bens bought. The old house on the place was in bad shape, but old houses certainly did make good homes in their better days. This old home must have been one of the better houses in the Clarita area at one time.

Ben was a farmer and also a carpenter. So he set to work and with time had a new house built. They moved into the basement at first and finished the rest of the house as they could. They put up a dairy barn and milked cows as well as working out as a carpenter.

Their buggy horse, Tony, was one of a kind. Good old Tony took Bens many a mile in the Clarita area. A very faithful horse.

Esther used a lot of sugar water each summer to feed the hummingbirds. They buzzed around the feeders continuously.

They planted fruit trees and a big garden. Esther was kept busy at home while Ben worked out after the building projects at home were done.

Ben J. Troyer, born February 25, 1943, was the son of John E. and Lydiann (Troyer) Troyer, grandson of Bishop Benjamin D. Troyer of Sugarcreek, Ohio. On October 29, 1964, he married Esther M. Miller, born November 7, 1942. She was the daughter of Moses J.B. and Emma J. (Hochstetler) Miller of Sugarcreek, Ohio.

Ben was ordained minister May 1, 1971 in the Sugarcreek, Ohio area.

Ben and Esther had a large wooded area where the wildflowers grew abundantly. The common poor-wills had their

The old house at Ben J. Troyers' farm had character. It must have been quite the house in its better days for the Clarita area.

nests there during the summer. One could hear their calls, poor-will, poor-will, as the evening shadows fell. During the summer the dickcissels flew up from the meadows and the wildlife roamed the woods. It was a nice place for the two boys to grow up in.

Children: Bruce was born October 21, 1965. On September 22, 1993, he married Esther Yoder in Wautoma, Wisconsin, at the age of 28. James was born June 19, 1972.

After living in Oklahoma for almost seventeen years Ben and Esther pulled up stakes and moved to Crab Orchard, Kentucky. Bruce was now living in Wautoma, Wisconsin, but James was still at home and moved with his parents to Kentucky on July 28, 1995. Bruce and his family moved to Crab Orchard later on. James is also married now and at the time of this writing he and his wife Lena and daughter Dorothy live in a portable house in Bens' yard and operate a woodworking shop.

They bought land and plan to build a new home soon. Ben and Bruce both do carpenter work and Esther operates Granny's Country Store which they built on their own property in the Crab Orchard area.

Ben is a brother to Melvin, #4.

Family #3—Crist & Fannie Yoder

Crist J.C. Yoder moved to Oklahoma from Millersburg Route 4 (the East Clark district), with his wife Fannie and six children on November 15, 1978. Crist was ordained minister on May 1, 1973, in the Clark area. So now there were three ministers living in the new Amish settlement near Clarita, Oklahoma.

Crist was born April 24, 1935. He was the son of John C. and Lydian M. (Raber) Yoder of Route 1, Baltic, Ohio.

He married December 6, 1956, to Fannie S. Troyer born June 12, 1936. She was the daughter of Simon P. and Mattie (Miller) Troyer of Route 4, Millersburg, Ohio.

Crist and most of his brothers raised Belgian draft horses and were known as good horsemen.

Crist was a farmer at heart, so he built a new barn and they milked cows and farmed.

They had school in their garage until a school was built or another place was ready.

Children

Eli	October 15, 1957
David	September 25, 1964
Mattie	July 30, 1967
Roy	September 28, 1971
Kathy	October 1, 1974

Crist J.C. and Fannie Yoder's farm from highway 48. Crists built the barn and farmed while living here.

Wayne   October 8, 1979—*Second Amish baby born in the Clarita settlement.*

Little Wayne had some health problems and was one of God's special children, a Down's baby. The summer of 1980 was an extra hot summer with nearly a month of everyday highs of 100° or over. With no air-conditioning and the health problems little Wayne had, the heat was about more than he could take.

And with row crops not being very successful in the Clarita area, with warm winds in the summer shriveling up the corn, Crist and Fannie decided to move to a cooler climate. So on June 9, 1981, they moved to Clare, Michigan.

Fannie is a sister to Mattie, #7.

Family #4— Melvin & Verna Troyer

Melvin was born December 24, 1949, to John E. and Lydiann (Troyer) Troyer. He married Verna Miller on March 13, 1969. She was born August 10, 1943, to Melvin A. and Mary J. (Miller) Miller.

Melvin J. Troyer moved his wife and family to Coal County, Oklahoma from the Sugarcreek, Ohio area on November 28, 1978.

Mels bought fifty acres near Clarita on the east side of the railroad track. There were no buildings on these acres. They bought and moved a house (the shell) from Ada, Oklahoma, then finished out the inside. They never unpacked their boxes (except clothes) until the house was finished. Until then they lived in a small trailer behind Raymonds' first place—now the Herman Stutzman farm—and put their boxes, etc. in Crist J.C. Yoders' garage.

As soon as they had built a barn they started milking cows. They also raised some hogs and Mel did carpenter

Melvin J. and Verna Troyer's farm. They lived here four years and had a dairy and raised hogs. Ten Amish families lived on this farm at one time or another. Joe Petersheims bought the fifty to fifty-one acres from Mel Troyers. Herman Stutzmans bought from Joes. Now David Yoders bought eighteen acres and the buildings and Hermans still own thirty-three acres.

work with his brother Ben J. Troyer.

Their school-age children went to Olney public school for awhile, then to Elm Creek where Mrs. Nettie Beiler was teacher. Carolyn was nine, Miriam seven, and Martha six that first winter.

Children

Carolyn	December 20, 1969
Miriam	September 18, 1971
Martha	October 7, 1972
Marie	February 17, 1974
Reuben	January 7, 1977

David   July 7, 1979

Wayne   October 17, 1981

David was the first Amish baby to be born in the Clarita Amish settlement, and Wayne was the third.

Mels lived in Oklahoma for four years, then moved back to Ohio in the Sugarcreek area in the fall of 1982. At the time of this writing they live in the Glenmont area in Ohio.

Melvin is a brother to Ben, #2.

Family #5—Norman & Sylvia Miller

It was another sub-zero day in December of 1978 at Rexford, Montana, when twenty-two-year-old Norman Miller started off to the bus station for a visit in the new community of Clarita, Oklahoma. On the way out he checked

Norman Miller bought an old house in Clarita and fixed it up and painted it. (Maybe the calf was a bonus.)

This is the house after Norman was finished. Here he brought his bride, Sylvia, after the wedding. This was the place where Vernon Millers, #17, lived in Clarita and Elmer Troyer, #24-A, bought from Vernons. Where Cristie, #29, and Mary Miller rented and lived for six months. Dan C. Masts, #6, bought it from Elmer Troyer then. After Dans moved it was no longer in Amish hands.

his mail. There was an invitation from his uncle Raymond Miller for Norman to come and visit. "I'm on my way, Uncle," were his thoughts as he continued on.

With the milder Oklahoma winters and plenty of work there, Norman bought an old house on four acres in the small town of Clarita, and moved there in January of 1979.

The following summer, ten youth from Mayes County accepted the invitation for a weekend visit in Coal County. This is how Norman met his future wife, Sylvia Yoder.

Norman was born November 29, 1956, to Emanuel and Mabel (Miller) Miller, Fresno, Ohio, and married April 9,

After moving back to Clarita, Norman and Sylvia built a new
house and barn at the north end of the settlement on forty acres
they bought from Willie Millers.

1981, to Sylvia Yoder, born October 2, 1962, daughter of
Levi and Cora Yoder, Inola, Oklahoma.

Norman fixed up and painted the old house he bought in
Clarita where the couple moved to after the wedding.

On December 30, 1981, Rachel Sue was born to them in
Ada, Oklahoma.

Norman did construction work with a crew on Federal
jobs part-time. In between he helped haul square bales and
did local carpenter work.

On February 16, 1982, Norman and Sylvia packed all
their belongings, including their horse Jerry, on a semi
and moved to Inola, Oklahoma (Rogers County), among
Sylvia's family. They sold their place to his brother, Vernon
Millers.

Normans later built a shop across the driveway from the house.
Here he keeps all his carpenter tools and needs.

Normans lived in Rogers County for five years. During
that time they operated a dairy on a rented farm and Norman did carpenter work.

With his heart still in Coal County, Norman and Sylvia,
with Rachel moved back on February 25, 1987. They bought
forty acres with several barns on it from Willie Millers. They
lived in one of the barns for six months, until their house
was built. They lived in the basement of the house and gradually finished out the main floor. Plans were to complete it
by spring of 1990.

But dreams and plans were shattered on February 23,
1990, when Rachel, now in second grade, started the daily
trip to Elm Creek School with Andy Millers' children. John
and Allen Jay were in the front seat. Rachel and Malinda
were in the back seat studying their memory verse, Mat-

A recent photo of Normans' place with all the landscaping done and flowers in bloom.

thew 6:33, when a grain truck came up from behind and hit the buggy. The horse, Bud, was killed instantly and the buggy exploded and flew to pieces, scattered about sixty feet along the road. The grain truck skidded an estimated three hundred feet and turned over on its side.

Rachel Sue had a severe head injury and was immediately unconscious. She had internal bleeding from head injuries as well as abdominal injuries, and was put on life support at the Ada Hospital and listed as very critical. But life support and medicine couldn't keep the brain swelling down. Early in the morning of February 24, Rachel went to be with the Lord. A large funeral was held at Elmer Yoders' large barn and Rachel was buried at the Amish cemetery, the second burial there.

With many a lonely day, Norman and Sylvia continued

Norman and Sylvia's cabin and pond where they enjoy bird-watching and fishing. In the spring one can see bluebirds and chickadees building nests in dead trees in the water in old woodpecker holes. Warblers are passing through and vireos perch high in the trees. Red-headed woodpeckers can be heard and seen scurrying up and down trees, while kingfishers and wild ducks come swooping down on the water, and turtles are sunning themselves lazily on the logs. As you travel in and out the path to the cabin, wild Rio Grande turkeys strut in full display.

with their lives. With plenty of carpenter jobs and building new houses, and remodeling, the days were kept busy for Norman. Sylvia did custom quilting the first years, but gradually there was more of a demand for piecing quilts for the annual school auction, which started in September of 1988.

Once again, during the summer of 2000, hearts were grieved when a lump in Norman's groin tested to be Hodgkins Disease. For six months, Norman took twelve chemo treatments in Ada, Oklahoma. By then the cancer was in remission, but an additional twenty radiation treatments were prescribed at M.D. Anderson in Houston, Texas during May of 2001.

Normans have some beef cattle which graze the pastures along with Andy the horse. They bought some land across the road along Boggy Creek and built a cabin in the wooded area, with a large pond in front. They enjoy bird-watching and wildlife. Norman also enjoys fishing, so the pond is stocked with fish. The Millers praise the Lord for His grace throughout the years and pray for His guiding hand into the future.

Joe & Lorene Schmucker

We would like to mention here that Joe and Lorene (Miller) Schmucker moved to Coleman, Oklahoma in January of 1979. They spent several winters there and came up to the Clarita settlement on Sundays for church services. They were from New Haven, Indiana, but have sold their property near Coleman, which is about twenty miles south of Clarita.

They were retired and did odd jobs. They came here instead of going to Florida for the winter months. But they don't come anymore.

Family #6—Dan & Verna Mast

Dan and Verna Mast moved to the Clarita settlement with their family in November of 1979. Dan was a polio victim and desired a warmer climate.

Daniel C. Mast, born on November 17, 1931, son of Christian J. and Lena F. (Nissley) Mast, Kalona, Iowa. He married on October 21, 1958, to Verna Mast who was born on October 7, 1931. She was the daughter of Emanuel and Mattie (Miller) Mast from Arthur, Illinois.

Dans moved to the Clarita settlement in Coal County on November 16, 1979.

Children

Chester Lee	September 5, 1959
Willis Ray	November 25, 1960
Lena Sue	October 17, 1962

The shop building on their place in Clarita where they set up the carpet loom.

Allen Duane	May 15, 1964
#27. Ruby Fern	March 20, 1966
David Leroy	July 28, 1967
Rosanna Fay	September 10, 1970
Wilma Arlene	July 5, 1972

Dan and Verna rented an old homestead in the southeast corner of the settlement. They milked cows and made rugs for a living. They set their loom up at the annual quilt auction and sold rugs. They made lots of rugs for the Amish as well as for others too.

They moved to Clarita after buying the house and property from Elmer Troyer. He had bought it from Vernon Millers. Here they set the loom up in the shop. The two youngest girls, Rosanna and Wilma, lived with them on this

The abandoned home where Dan and Verna Mast used to live on the back road at the southeast end of the settlement. From here they moved to the little white house in Clarita.

property. The two oldest girls, Lena and Ruby, were married and lived in Iowa.

Dans moved to Bloomfield, Iowa on September 12, 1995. Dans are parents to Ruby, #27.

Family #6-A

Dan's mother, Lena, a widow, came to live with Dans on October 24, 1980. Lena was the wife of Christian J. Mast, born May 22, 1897, and died on November 26, 1972. Lena was born January 20, 1897. Christian and Lena were both born in Kansas and later moved to Kalona, Iowa.

Children

	Fannie	March 8, 1920
	Elizabeth	December 12, 1921
	Leander	September 5, 1924
	Anna	December 24, 1927
#6.	Daniel	November 17, 1931
	Moses	March 17, 1936

Lena died on December 27, 1985. The funeral was at Dan Masts on December 29, 1985. The body was then taken to Kalona, Iowa for another funeral and burial.

Family #7—Melvin J. Hershbergers

In the fall of 1979, Melvin and his wife Mattie decided to buy a farm in the new Amish settlement in Clarita, Oklahoma. Holmes County was getting more crowded and Melvin was thinking of room to expand for future families. He liked the idea of grazing and grasslands.

On February 19, 1980, the Hershbergers moved to Coal County, Oklahoma. They had bought 160 acres and built a dairy barn that first summer. A year later they bought fifty acres more. They had brought along some dairy heifers from Holmes County to start a dairy herd. They milked an average of forty cows when they started milking and built their herd up to a big herd.

After the boys had all left home Melvins decided to sell the dairy herd in 1998. They now have a herd of beef cattle (Brangus and Angus) which they graze on their fields during the summer. In the winter they feed hay out in the open fields. They still make their own hay.

The first year they lived there they sold baked goods, honey, and cheese from the house. In 1982, they built a little country store. Here they still sell baked goods, honey, bulk foods, gifts, souvenirs, and straw hats. Cookbooks are big

Melvin and Mattie Hershberger's house. The children have all gone from home now except Fannie. She helps Mattie bake for their store and helps with the housework.

Melvins' country store where they sell honey, baked goods, cheese, bulk food, gifts, souvenirs, straw hats, and cookbooks. They are located just off highway 48 north of Wapanucka. They have a sign out by the highway.

sellers too. They usually sell a lot of baked goods and cookbooks at the annual school auction.

Their country store seems to be a success. The fresh baked goods are a treat for the native Okies and also the people traveling through the area with a lot of them coming from Texas.

Fannie is still helping at home, and the rest of the children are either married or moved away.

Melvin J. Hershberger was born March 12, 1939. He was the son of Jacob E. and Fannie (Miller) Hershberger of Route 5, Millersburg, Ohio (Bunker Hill area). He married on December 3, 1959, to Mattie S. Troyer, who was born August 19, 1938. She was the daughter of Simon P. and

The Melvin Hershberger farm. They had a dairy for many years, but now since the boys have all left home, Melvin has beef cows and helps run their country store.

Mattie (Miller) Troyer of Route 4, Millersburg, Ohio.
  Children
  #28. Ada   November 12, 1960
       Fannie   October 18, 1961
  #25. Mary   September 10, 1964
  #26. Abe   February 19, 1966
       Mose   March 15, 1971
       Andrew   October 25, 1973
       Esther   January 7, 1976

Lone Star School was in Melvins' back yard and both Ada and Mary taught school there.

Mattie is a sister to Fannie, #3, and parent to Mary, #25,

Abe, #26, and Ada, #28.

Family #8—Ben & Alma Hostetler

Ben W. Hostetler was born January 2, 1916. He was the son of William and Sarah (Kauffman) Hostetler of the Mt. Eaton area. He married December 14, 1939, to Alma Beachy. She was born February 9, 1918, the daughter of Bishop Albert and Katie (Miller) Beachy of the Sugarcreek, Ohio area.

Ben and Alma moved to Coal County, Oklahoma on February 23, 1980, the same day as Menno and Irene Yoder.

Children

	Edna	October 3, 1940
	Lovina	October 20, 1941
#1.	Elsie	May 30, 1943
	Freeman	July 23, 1944

Ben and Alma Hostetler's house and garden. Edwin and Esther Miller now live here. The old house is gone and a new one built.

#9. Irene	April 12, 1946
Henry	July 20, 1947
William	November 2, 1949
Albert	July 31, 1951
Benj. Jr.	January 13, 1953
Vernon	October 19, 1954
Edwin	November 17, 1955
Katie	November 25, 1957

Bens are the parents of Elsie, #1, and Irene, #9. They moved back to Ohio on June 1, 1987.

Family #9—Menno E. Yoders

It was on the twenty-third day of February 1980, when Menno E. Yoder and wife, Irene, with their three children, Jonathan ten, Kathryn eight, and James seven, left their home near Sugarcreek, Ohio, and moved to Coal County, Oklahoma to the new Amish settlement.

Irene's parents, family #8, moved with the Yoders to a smaller house on the same property.

There was an old farmhouse on the Yoders' farm but it wasn't in good shape, so the Yoders built a new house and moved into the basement. The roof and sides were finished on the main floor of the house but the partitions were not put in right away.

The three children went to Olney public school at first, since they lived near Olney. Later on they fixed up a room in the old farmhouse for a schoolroom. The children at that end of the settlement went to school there with Lena Mast as teacher. Lena was Dan C. Masts' daughter and was nineteen at the time. The school was named Hardwood School and had fourteen pupils.

The Yoders experienced an extra hot summer that first year with nearly a month of 100-degree plus weather. But despite the heat wave they adjusted well. Irene felt right at home and enjoyed the smaller community where everyone was friendly and life was more simple. Irene was a sister to Elsie, #1.

One day as Irene was on her way home from Dan Masts where she had been to help Verna get ready for church, a black cloud came up very quickly. It was churning and rolling low. Tornado clouds! The buggy started rocking back and forth and the horse refused to go on. Finally the cloud passed on.

When Irene got home the storm had blown the roof and sides of their new house over. But with the help of the com-

The Menno Yoder farm. The old house where they held school classes (Hardwood), and where Menno and Irene worked in their harness shop is no longer there.

munity men, the walls were erected again and the roof put back on. But this time they put the partitions in to help support the walls.

Menno was born August 1, 1945, son of Emanuel J. and Gertie (Beachy) Yoder of Star Route, Millersburg (at Route 39 near Berlin). On November 7, 1968, he married Irene B. Hostetler, born April 12, 1946, daughter of Benj. W. Hostetler. To this union were born five children.

Jonathan	October 4, 1969
Kathryn	July 5, 1971
James	June 14, 1972
Joseph	December 4, 1976 - died Dec. 4, 1976
Susan Marie	September 2, 1988

In October of 1981, something happened that wasn't soon forgotten by the Coal County, Oklahoma residents. It rained and rained and rained. It just poured down and the Ohioans had never seen it rain like this before. It kept on raining, totaling twenty-four to twenty-five inches in a week. The creeks overflowed and the low spots flooded. The swift current washed away the rural waterline that crossed Boggy Creek to the Clarita, Olney area. This left homes without running water, but there was plenty of rain water roaring down the creeks.

During this rainstorm Menno and the three children had quite an experience coming home from school. This year Hardwood School (Lena Mast teacher) and Ash Flats (Ada Hershberger teacher) and Elm Creek (Mrs. Nettie Beiler teacher) combined to one school at Melvin Hershbergers. Menno had taken the children to school that first rainy morning, not thinking that there wouldn't be any school.

When they got there school was closed, so they turned around and went back home. It rained so hard and fast, that by the time he came closer to home at the corner of 31B, close to the bridge, the horse wouldn't go on as the water was rising fast and getting deep. Menno got out and put the children one by one on the fence where they held on to the fence posts for dear life. Then Menno unhitched the horse and tied the buggy to the fence. He put the battery on the seat, and told the horse to go home after he put up the lines and loosened the reins.

Just then Don Lawrence came along and helped Menno get the children off the fence. Don took James on his shoulder and Menno took Kathryn. They each held on to Jonathan who was between them. Together they waded the flooding waters and with the good Lord's help, arrived safely home to an anxious Irene who didn't know what happened with Menno and the children when the horse came home alone. Kathryn's school bonnet was lost in the high water and washed down the creek, never to be found again. But all's well that ends well.

Menno worked for Gus Martin on the Hereford ranch part-time. They also had a dairy and milked cows once they got set up. They also had a harness shop which they had in part of the old house. Irene worked in there a lot. Menno had a welding shop too. Later they sold the harness inventory, etc. to Mart Hochstetlers in May of 1985.

On May 22, 1985, Menno took his family back to Ohio to the West Union community in the southern part of the state where two of his sisters and families lived.

Irene is a sister to Elsie, #1, and daughter to #8.

Family #10—John B. Beachys

John and Mary Beachy moved to Coal County, Oklahoma in the spring of 1980, from Bunker Hill North district in Holmes County, Ohio. It was on May 6 when they unloaded at the farm they bought, what we now know as the Herman Yoder farm. Johnnys bought this place from Mel Troyers, although Mels had never lived on the farm.

John B. Beachy was born October 21, 1945. He was the son of Ben B. and Katie (Raber) Beachy of Holmes County, Ohio. On November 12, 1968, he married to Mary Schrock who was born October 14, 1949. She was the daughter of Crist A. and Lizzie Ann (Beachy) Schrock of Berlin, Ohio.

John was ordained minister on May 3, 1975, and ordained bishop on October 1, 1977.

Children
Edward Allen	August 29, 1969
Benjamin Ray	June 23, 1971
Katherine Ann	February 4, 1973
Linda	December 16, 1976

John built a welding shop and put out some crops. They were unfortunate to have moved just before that very warm summer when the heat dried up their crop. Temperatures soared up over 100° a lot of the time, which didn't help matters any. The children went to school at Menno Yoders' old house (Hardwood School). Edward was eleven, Ben nine, and Katherine seven that school term. Linda was four that winter and still at home.

By the next spring, on May 21, 1981, John took his family back to Ohio. They built a new home on five acres of land close to where they had lived before moving to Oklahoma.

Menno Yoder took over the welding shop after Johns left.

Family #11—Ben B. Troyers

Ben and Emma Troyer moved from Lakeside, Ontario, Canada on October 31, 1980. Ben and Emma are originally from Hartville, Ohio. They moved to Coal County, Oklahoma with their family and Emma's parents (#12) on a farm at the north end of the settlement.

Ben was born on August 21, 1938, son of Ben and Amanda (Beachy) Troyer. He married Emma Mast on September 21, 1960. She was born September 12, 1939, daughter of Ezra and Anna (Miller) Mast. Ben was ordained minister April 9, 1972, at Chaco, Paraguay, S.A. He was ordained bishop in October of 1976, at Lakeside, Ontario, Canada.

Children

Joni	November 23, 1961
#47. Daniel	August 9, 1963
Melvin	January 14, 1965
#41. Levi	July 6, 1967
#40. Esther	April 29, 1969
Laura	July 6, 1971
#48. John	October 24, 1973

Laura married Paul Kemp on March 29, 1995, and moved to Milroy, Indiana on April 10, 1995. They had a son Marlin, born on May 6, 1992, died on December 19, 1999.

Bens' 278-acre farm was up on a little rise. You could see a long ways over the prairie from here. They had a dairy farm and milked cows. The boys worked out some. Hauled hay and did carpenter work. They also did farm work for local farmers and ranchers (non-Amish).

Bens moved to Dublin, Texas on November 29, 1983, to

Ben B. and Emma Troyer's house on their 278-acre farm.

Here are some of the dogs Bens raise in the outside pens.

Ben and Emma Troyer's farm looking southwest—Mart Hochstetlers' farm buildings are in the trees in the center across the road. Beyond Marts' place is Andy Millers' house. Way in the background to the right is the Clarita water tower in Clarita and to the left is Doyle Nelsons' farm. This is the place where the annual school auction has been for the last eight years. In this photo you can see that Noah and Anna Coblentz's house is right beside Ben and Emma's.

work on a dairy farm. They moved back to their farm in the Clarita settlement on February 21, 1991. They milked cows again after coming back from Texas until five years ago when they quit the dairy. Ben had beef cows and worked part-time with Elmer Yoder Construction until Elmers moved away. Now the last two years they raise dogs and turned their milk barn into dog kennels and the milk house into a whelping house. Emma tends to the dogs—lots of work involved. Ben works with John Henry Miller's crew, and goes to work at 6:00 in the morning.

Some of the dogs they raise are Bernice Mountain, Cav-

These are the Bernice Mountain dogs that are so expensive.

This is the inside of Ben B.'s dairy barn that has been turned into dog kennels. The milk house has been turned into a whelping house. Emma takes care of the dogs while Ben works on the carpenter crew. She does a lot of paperwork for the dogs too.

ilier King Charles, Minipins, Bischon Frise, Pomeranians, Chihuahuas, and Rat Terriers.

When driving in their driveway there are no more cattle by the cattle guard. As you get close to the buildings, there is no question what they raise. Dogs seem to be barking everywhere. Some in the barn and others out back in large pens.

Emma does a lot of paperwork on the dogs too and still finds time to quilt. She is a daughter to Anna, #12, and an aunt to Nettie, #13, Anna Mary, #20, and Clara, #21.

Bens have had the annual school auction at their farm for the last eight years now.

Family #12—Noah J. Coblentzs

Noah J. Coblentz was born December 31, 1897, and died November 29, 1992, at the age of 94 years, 10 months, and 29 days. He was the son of Joe D. and Anna (Troyer) Coblentz of Hartville, Ohio. He married Lydiann Schlabach on December 25, 1919, who was born December 13, 1900, and died October 17, 1949. She was a daughter of Christ D. and Mary (Raber) Schlabach.

Noah was ordained minister May 10, 1937, and ordained bishop May 31, 1941, in Stark County, Ohio.

Children of Noah and Lydiann

Orin	May 5, 1921
Daniel	December 22, 1923
Anna Mary	October 29, 1925
Esther	May 22, 1930
Earl	December 15, 1931
Emma	November 18, 1933
John Henry	June 7, 1936
Vernon	August 22, 1937

Amanda	May 8, 1939
Nettie	May 28, 1941
Roy	October 26, 1942
Joe	November 21, 1943

Noah was married the second time December 22, 1950, to Anna (Miller) Mast. They moved to Coal County, Oklahoma from Lakeside, Ontario, Canada with Ben B. Troyers on October 31, 1980. After Bens and Noahs came, the new Amish settlement in Clarita had three bishops and three ministers and was only two years old.

Noah's second wife, Anna (Miller) Mast, was born September 14, 1910, and married the first time on December 6, 1928, to Ezra Mast who was born August 14, 1903, and died January 2, 1946, near Mercer, Pennsylvania. Anna was the

Noah and Anna Coblentz's house where they lived on Ben B. and Emma Troyer's farm, beside Bens' house. Emma is Anna Coblentz's daughter.

daughter of John N. and Fannie (Troyer) Miller of Hartville, Ohio. Anna died in the Clarita settlement on January 23, 2002, and is buried in Hartville, Ohio.

Children of Ezra and Anna

	Fannie	April 4, 1931
	Edna	October 1, 1932
	Levi	February 19, 1936
11.	Emma	September 12, 1939
	John	May 28, 1941

Anna was a grandmother to quite a few of the young families living in Coal County. She was grandmother to all of Bens' children there and #13, #20, and #21. She was known to all in the settlement as "mommy". Some still say "Oklahoma mommy" when referring to her. She quilted a lot of quilts and did a fine job except towards the last when her eyes weren't so good anymore. Noah threaded her needles and she quilted day after day.

Noah had beef cows at first when they moved, but later he sold them and just threaded needles and did other small jobs. Every day he faithfully went out the lane to get "die posht" (the mail). You could almost set your clock by him. If the mailman was on time he was too.

Family #13—Andrew Beilers

Andrew B. Beiler, born May 2, 1953, son of John and Savilla (Blank) Beiler of Lancaster, Pennsylvania. He married on December 20, 1979, to Nettie Detweiler, born April 29, 1958. She was the daughter of Bishop John and Fannie (Mast) Detweiler of Marion, Kentucky.

They moved to Coal County, Oklahoma on March 11, 1981. They stayed with her grandparents, Noah Coblentzs, until they found another place to live. After John Beachys moved back to Ohio they rented the Herman Yoder place before Hermans moved there. After Hermans moved they had to move again, so Andrew took his family to Coleman, Oklahoma where he farmed some and had goats.

Andrew had a pioneer spirit and after their wedding he took his bride to Roanoke, Virginia in a covered wagon. He had originally planned to go to Pennsylvania with his family, but decided en route to stay at Roanoke. From there they came to Oklahoma.

Children:

Marie Mae	January 5, 1981
Joseph Ray	March 17, 1983

Andy and Nettie moved to Texas (Dublin) on October 16, 1984, and raised dogs there. Later in 1997 he moved his family to Paraguay, South America.

Nettie is a sister to Anna Mary, #20, and Clara, #21, a granddaughter to Anna Coblentz, #12, and a niece to Emma, #11.

Family #14—Lonnie Millers

Lonnie F. Millers moved to Coal County, Oklahoma from Centerville, Michigan on December 15, 1981. Lonnie was born October 6, 1903, the son of Feneas D. and Fanny J. (Stutzman) Miller of Newton County, Indiana. He married Polly P. Miller on January 28, 1926. She was born October 10, 1903, the daughter of Peter E. and Elizabeth (Troyer) Miller of Centerville. They stayed at Ben B. Troyers until they built something to move into.

Children

Twin sons	September 20, 1926 - Stillborn

This building is where Lonnie and Polly Miller lived. They lived in the one on the right.

#15.	William L.	March 25, 1931
	Clarence L.	June 17, 1932 - August 12, 1978
	Elizabeth L.	June 2, 1935 - January 28, 1965
	Perry L.	November 23, 1938 - September 17, 1965
	Vernon Leroy	March 1, 1944 - March 5, 1944

Lonnie and Polly moved to Dublin, Texas on May 9, 1983. They returned to the Clarita settlement on December 7, 1984. Polly died March 13, 1985, and was taken to Centerville, Michigan for burial. Lonnie stayed in Centerville for awhile. He passed away while at Shipshewana, Indiana on November 14, 1989, at his son Williams. He had lived with them since July of 1986.

Family #15—Willie and Sarah Miller

William L. Miller, born March 25, 1931, son of Lonnie F.

The building on the left is where Willie and Sarah Miller lived. These buildings are still in use on the Norman Miller place. Normans lived in the same building Willies did after adding an addition, until their new house was built. They now use it for their barns.

and Polly (Miller) Miller, married March 10, 1955 to Sarah Miller, born September 21, 1930. She was a daughter to Andrew and Anna (Burkholder) Miller of Nappanee, Indiana.

Willie and Sarah moved with his parents, Lonnie and Polly, to Coal County, Oklahoma from Centerville, Michigan on December 15, 1981.

They bought some land from a local farmer, Larry Patton, at the north end of the settlement. There were no buildings, so they both stayed with Ben B. Troyers until they had built some sheds to move into.

Willie was ordained minister March 28, 1969, in Paraguay, South America by Bishop Noah Coblentz. They had no children. They moved to Dublin, Texas from Clarita to work on a dairy and didn't return to Clarita, but moved to Middlebury, Indiana from Texas in August 1986.

Family #16—Atlee & Fannie Stutzman

Atlee Stutzman, son of Emery H. and Fannie (Weaver) Stutzman of Milroy, Indiana, married October 11, 1962, to Ida Detweiler who was born October 24, 1938. She was the daughter of Bishop Tobias J. and Lena (Miller) Detweiler of Jamesport, Missouri.

Atlee and Fannie and their family moved to Coal County, Oklahoma from Jamesport, Missouri on February 3, 1982. They bought land at the south end of the settlement and Atlee built a dairy barn and they farmed.

Children

     Sylvia   April 16, 1964

This is the dairy barn Atlee Stutzman built. They lived in a trailer, but the trailer is no longer there.

John Emery	December 7, 1965
Barbara Ann	July 11, 1967
David Leroy	May 31, 1968
Harvey	December 22, 1969
Joseph Wayne	January 6, 1971
Elizabeth	April 9, 1972 - June 3, 1972
Ada Mae	November 2, 1973
Erma	June 20, 1975
Atlee Jr.	March 25, 1977
Rachel	May 22, 1978 - Stillborn
Aaron Ray	June 9, 1979

Atlees moved to Dublin, Texas in December 1983, and moved back to Jamesport, Missouri in September of 1985. Atlee is a brother to John Henry, #21.

Family #17—Vernon Millers
Vernon and Esta Miller moved to Clarita, Oklahoma from Fresno, Ohio (New Bedford area) on February 20, 1982. Vernon E. Miller, born October 14, 1954, is the son of Bishop Emanuel D. and Mabel (Miller) Miller of the Fresno, Ohio area. He married June 2, 1977 to Esta Troyer, born December 5, 1952, daughter of Elmer and Katie (Schlabach) Troyer.
Children

Jeremy	May 29, 1978
Leona	June 19, 1980
Steven	September 29, 1982

Vernons bought the property in the little town of Clarita that belonged to his brother Normans, when Normans moved back to Inola, among Sylvia's family.

Vernon started a shop, making and repairing buggies. He added on and made it bigger by 1985, and also had orders for making and redoing covered wagons (Conestoga). There was a big wagon train going through Texas sometime in the summer of 1985. One covered wagon Vernon did was sponsored by Wrangler Jeans for the wagon train. Esta sewed the canvas for the top. It looked like the real thing.

Vernons bought land (fifteen acres) from Mart and Susan Hochstetler and started building a new buggy shop and house in May of 1987. Here they continued with the carriage business until they moved back to Ohio on July 25, 1990. Bobby Bear moved them to Ohio.

Vernon is a nephew to Raymond, #1, and a brother to Norman, #5. Esta is a sister to Susan, #24.

Vernons had the annual school auction at their place for the first two years.

This is the Clarita Carriage Shop at Vernon Millers' place in Clarita before they moved to the new place (present-day photo).

Vernon and Esta's new house on the fifteen acres they bought from Mart Hochstetelers' farm.

The new carriage shop Vernons built is now partially hidden by one of the pines they planted. This photo was taken twelve years after Vernons moved away.

Mel Ray and Liz Miller bought Vernon and Esta's house, shop, and the fifteen acres and moved in the same day Vernons moved out.

Family #18—Melvin Ray Millers

Melvin and Elizabeth (Liz) Miller moved to Coal County, Oklahoma from Nappanee, Indiana on May 14, 1982. Melvin Ray was born May 6, 1959. He was the son of Jonas and Ruth (Kauffman) Miller of Nappanee, Indiana. He married Elizabeth Ann Bontrager on November 3, 1977. She was born January 13, 1957, a daughter to Monroe and Mary (Schrock) Bontrager of Millersburg, Indiana.

Children

Loretta	Stillborn
Jonas Lee	May 10, 1979
Marilyn Sue	September 18, 1980
Rose Ann	June 26, 1985
Jolene	July 19, 1986

Mel Ray used the shop for his cabinet shop the nine years they lived in the Clarita settlement.

Esther Marie   July 29, 1987
Reuben James   September 15, 1989
Daniel Ray   December 24, 1991
Melvin Monroe   June 13, 1994

Mel Rays first lived in the old house behind Herman Stutzmans (across the creek). He tried to start a cabinet shop but didn't have the equipment plus business was slow. So they went to Stephenville, Texas to work on a dairy, after living in the Clarita settlement for eleven months. They left for Texas before Raymonds, Bens, and Willies. They had left only a month when Willies followed.

Mel Rays were on a dairy for one and a half years when he started a cabinet shop again in Texas. On July 24, 1990, they moved back to Clarita on the property Vernon Millers vacated when they moved back to Ohio. There they had Vernons' nice, big, almost new shop for a cabinet shop. At first they refinished old furniture besides making cabinets. They were in the cabinet business for nine years. The last two years they made cabinets mostly for Indiana housing.

Mel Rays moved to Haven, Kansas on February 17, 1999. Their son Jonas is married now and lives in Indiana, and daughter Marilyn is married to Andrew Knepp and lives in Haven too. Mel Rays had their tenth child after living in Haven, named Rebecca. She is two years old at this writing. Mel Ray is the son of Jonas, #36.

Family #19—Herman Yoders

Herman Ray and Ida Yoder moved to Coal County, Oklahoma from Inola, Oklahoma (Chouteau) on December 28, 1982.

Herman was born on September 27, 1948, to John A. Jr.

Herman and Ida Yoder's house. They remodeled the inside and added on to the original house.

Herman put up a dairy barn and other sheds as well. The old mower in the foreground is a relic of bygone days.

and Bertha (Yoder) Yoder of Garnett, Kansas. He married on October 22, 1970, to Ida Yoder, a daughter to Bishop Melvin N. and Edna S. (Miller) Yoder of Chouteau. Ida was born on August 11, 1945.

Children

#37. Heidi Ellen	July 17, 1971
#42. Lori Ann	April 6, 1973
Tobias Jay	July 10, 1976
Sara Faye	September 16, 1979
Claire Kay	July 17, 1981
Ida Ruth	May 20, 1985

Herman built a dairy barn and they milked cows. Heidi and Lori were his milkmaids. When Tobias was old enough he helped on the farm too. They also raised hogs. Herman drove a matching team of Arabian horses which he also used in the fields. He made lots of hay for his dairy cows, calves, and heifers.

They remodeled the house and added on to it. Their youngest daughter, Ruth, had an accident while playing on the farm when she was about five years old. They rushed her to Coalgate where she was life-flighted to Oklahoma City Hospital. She survived the accident, but took quite awhile to recover.

Hermans moved to Kalona, Iowa on August 24, 1994. Their children are all married now except Ida Ruth, and all of them live in Kalona at the time of this writing. Herman Ida is bothered with rheumatoid arthritis.

Ida is an aunt to Sylvia, #5, Allen, #25, Lydia Anne, #26, Mary, #29, and Anna Marie, #43.

Hermans are parents to Heidi, #37, and Lori, #42.

Family #20—Elmer and Anna Mary Yoder

Elmer Yoder, Jr. was born February 3, 1951. He was the son of Deacon Elmer and Anna (Mast) Yoder of St. Mary's, Ontario, Canada. He was married to Anna Mary Detweiler on April 5, 1979. She was born on June 13, 1951, to Bishop John and Fannie (Mast) Detweiler of Marion, Kentucky.

Elmer and Anna Mary and son Wayne moved to Coal County, Oklahoma on June 9, 1983. They first moved on the Mel Troyer place near Clarita. Then when Ben B. Troyers moved to Texas, they moved into Bens' house beside her grandparents, Noah and Anna Coblentz.

Elmer had a carpenter crew, Yoder Construction, which employed a number of Amish in the community. They owned land out along Route 48. Later they hired Andy

Elmers lived in Ben B. and Emma's house while Bens were in Texas.

The big barn where Elmers lived before they put up their basement house.

A view of Elmers' pond south of the basement house. A perfect spot for purple martin housing. The great blue heron and the Canada geese also enjoy the pond.

Miller and boys and the rest of Elmer's crew to build a barn and shop combination. Andys then lived in the shop part first, then Elmers moved in later on after Andys built a home of their own.

Elmers had the annual school auction at their place for five years. The big barn came in handy for this with tents set up besides.

Elmers built a basement house and a pond south of the house. The purple martin house by the pond attracts the martins each year.

Anna Mary is a sister to Nettie, #13, Clara, #21, and a granddaughter to Anna, #12, a niece to Emma, #11. All of these lived in Paraguay, South America at one time and had many stories to tell about their life there.

The basement house as it looked when Elmers lived there.

Children of Elmer and Anna Mary

Wayne Allen	February 13, 1980
Michael John	August 16, 1983
Matthew Yost	August 16, 1983
Rachel Irene	October 27, 1986

Elmers moved to Mt. Vernon, Missouri on June 23, 1995.

Family #21—John Henry & Clara Stutzman

John Henry Stutzman was born February 21, 1959. He is the son of Emery H. and Fannie (Weaver) Stutzman of Milroy, Indiana. He married Clara Detweiler on September 23, 1982. She is the daughter of Bishop John and Fannie (Mast) Detweiler from Marion, Kentucky. Clara was born

John Henrys' house after adding an upstairs and remodeling the original house.

on September 28, 1960.

John Henrys first moved to Oklahoma in July of 1983, from Milroy, Indiana. They worked on a farm close to Durant. In May of 1984, they moved to Stephenville, Texas, where some of the other families had moved to. From there they moved to West Union, Ohio in the summer of 1985. In October of 1986, they came to Clarita, Oklahoma and stayed at Elmer Yoders for several weeks. Clara helped Anna Mary with household duties after Elmers' Rachel was born. Then they moved on to Sulphur Springs, Texas and worked there until April 16, 1990, when they moved back to the Clarita settlement. They moved to the south end, closer to Melvin Hershbergers. He did carpenter work first. There they remodeled and added an upstairs to the house and built a long calf barn, where Clara and the boys worked.

The calf barn they built to raise calves. Clara did the chores and the boys helped.

Clara also quilted. She is a sister to Nettie, #13, Anna Mary, #20, granddaughter to Anna, #12, and a niece to Emma, #11. John Henry is a brother to Atlee, #16.

Children

| Monroe Allen | September 22, 1983 |
| Marvin | December 21, 1984 |

They moved to Crab Orchard, Kentucky on March 23, 1995, and still live there at the time of this writing. John Henry has had health problems. He has had heart problems for a good many years, had surgeries, put in pacemakers, etc.

Family #22—Herman & Dorothy Stutzman

The old house where Herman and Dorothy lived until they built the new one. This is also where Raymond Millers lived before they moved to Texas.

Herman and Dorothy Stutzman and family moved to Coal County, Oklahoma from Jamesport, Missouri on September 28, 1983.

Herman was born June 17, 1944, to Noah J. and Fannie (Yoder) Stutzman of Garnett, Kansas. He married Dorothy Irene Petersheim on January 4, 1968. She was born March 8, 1948, to Joe and Mattie (Yoder) Petersheim of Haven, Kansas.

Hermans moved on the Raymond Miller farm and started a dairy. They brought dairy cows along from Jamesport and milked cows for almost twenty years. The three oldest were boys and helped on the farm. They raised hogs too. When the boys grew up and got married the two girls were the milkmaids. Hermans milked cows until February of 2003.

Herman and Dorothy's new house.

They raised good alfalfa hay and farmed the Mel Troyer place part-time.

They bought the Mel Troyer place from Joe Petersheim when Joe bought the Robinson place from Herman Yoder. (Joe had bought the Troyer place from Mels.)

In the spring of 1985, Hermans planted five acres of okra. They planted it on May 9. Lydia Yoder from Chouteau came to help in the okra patch. The first picking was July 8. They picked 100 pounds that time. They kept increasing until they picked 694 pounds in a day. They picked through August and spent many a day in the summer heat in the okra patch. Allen McHenrick came and got the okra and took it to market in Atoka.

Children

| #37. David Leon | April 27, 1969 |
| #42. Jacob Wayne | July 12, 1970 |

A summer view of Herman's new buildings and Dorothy's garden. She was a good gardener.

#46. Herman Joe	September 20, 1972
Miriam Sue	July 15, 1976
Nathan Lee	August 23, 1978
Rachel Ann	June 13, 1982

After the dairy cows were sold, Hermans got beef cows to graze the pastures. They now raise calves which they get from two different dairies in Texas. They kept three Holstein cows to milk. They use the milk to feed the calves. They get from twelve to fifteen calves at a time.

Dorothy plants their (early) garden in mid February. She has lots of spring flowers planted around the house which bloom in late February or early March.

In Hermans' back yard they have shelties penned up which they raise. They also have a few peacocks and doves.

The chicken pen is back there too, where they keep enough hens for their own eggs.

Herman and Dorothy also bought the Davidson place that joins their farm to the north.

Family #23—Andy & Mary Miller

Andy A. Miller, Jr. was born May 28, 1946. He is a son to Andy and Katie Y. (Mast) Miller of Dover, Delaware. On October 5, 1967, he married Mary D. Yoder. She was born March 27, 1946, to Bishop Dan A. and Malinda A. (Miller) Yoder of Dover, Delaware.

Children of Andy and Mary
      Kathryn Lorene   July 1, 1968
      Steven Ray   October 2, 1970

A view of Andy and Mary Miller's home from highway 48. The wild geese fly into the pasture fields by the flocks to enjoy the first green grass of spring.

These Brahma-cross cattle graze in the field just south of Andys.
These cattle are able to endure a warm and dry climate better and
are more resistant to ticks and other parasites.

#38. Andrew   May 28, 1972
     Amos   February 8, 1975
     John   December 29, 1976
     Malinda   March 28, 1980
     Allen Jay   December 1, 1982

Andys moved to Coal County, Oklahoma from the Milton, Iowa area on March 24, 1984. They first rented at
the Atlee Stutzman place (now Abe Hershbergers) Andy
worked part-time for Elmer Yoder and also at times for Joe
Shutte. In August 1984 until August of 1985, they lived at
the Mel Troyer place just before school started and worked
for Doyle Nelson on his dairy. In August of 1985 they

What used to be the Andy Miller home now has a completely different appearance. Double porches and high pillars give a different look. The washhouse looks the same.

moved to the Menno Yoder place and rented there until April of 1986 when Allen Yoders got married and moved on that farm. After the wedding of Allen and Mary, Andys moved to the north end of the community on Elmer Yoders' place in the shop part of the new barn that Andy and his boys put up for Elmer.

After they were settled in Andy worked for Elmer Yoder's construction crew. His wife Mary and their daughter Kathryn baked a variety of baked goods to sell out by the road along Route 48. They started baking around Easter time and baked until Thanksgiving. After school was out some of the younger children helped too.

The oldest boys worked with Yoder's Construction crew when they were out of school and old enough.

The barn at Elmers where Andys lived before building their own home.

In the fall after the first frost, Kathryn and whoever else in the family that wasn't busy elsewhere or going to school, helped Bobby Woods with the pecan harvest. Sometimes Kathryn helped Ann Woods in the greenhouse at the peak of the season.

Later Kathryn worked in Mel Ray's cabinet shop for one year. She bought the dry goods store from Joe Masts the spring after Andrews got married.

Andys bought thirty acres along Route 48 from Elmer Yoders. In 1989, they built a house of their own on that property. They moved there the first part of February 1990. Just two weeks later the accident occurred on highway 48 when Andys' three youngest children started out for school one morning with Normans' eight-year-old Rachel along.

John had ligaments torn in his legs and back. Malinda had a broken leg and elbow. Allen Jay had a skull fracture and had it overlapped and healed that way. A month later he had to have surgery to correct it. That accident was a shock to the whole community. A tragedy the Clarita settlement and all who were involved will always remember. It claimed the life of Normans' only child. Only God knows why.

Andys wrote this poem in memory of Rachel on her birthday and at Christmas time.

We are thinking of you, Dear Rachel,
As your birthday time draws near;
How we'd love to give you a card,
Filled with lots of love and cheer.

We miss you, Rachel, and even tho'
Our tears at times just want to flow,
We know you've reached that mansion fair,
That Jesus promised to prepare.

Loved ones on that happy shore,
Live forever, their tears are over,
For Heaven's shore will far outweigh,
Anything this earth to us conveys.

God looked around His garden, and saw an empty place,
He looked down upon the earth, and saw your sweet face;
He put His arms around you, and lifted you to rest,
God's garden must be beautiful, for He only takes the best.

Rachel dear, we miss you in the morning,
When it's time to leave for school;
You used to come bouncing in,
And all our hearts you did win.

On the way to school that fatal morning,
The truck hit them without warning;
The two little girls, in the back seat,
Were helping each other their memory verse to repeat.

The verse for the week was Matthew 6:33,
Which were the last words that Rachel did say.
Oh, what nice words, for when the Lord is nigh,
To take her up to the Angels on High.

And though we cannot see the ones
With whom we have to part,
Their memory, like a melody,
Still lingers in our hearts.

Gone but not forgotten.
Our loss is her gain.

Andys moved to West Union, Ohio on May 15, 1995.
Andys are parents to Andrew, #38.

Family #24—Martin & Susan Hochstetler

Martin J. Hochstetler was born to Jonas M. and Anna (Miller) Hochstetler on July 27, 1940, near Apple Creek, Ohio. He married Susan Irene Troyer on May 7, 1970, near Holmesville, Ohio. She was a daughter to Elmer M. and Katie (Schlabach) Troyer, and was born on June 23, 1947.

Children

Steven	May 21, 1971
Edwin	April 16, 1973

On Monday April 22, 1985, the red shanty was loaded onto a semi flatbed again and filled with Mart and Susan's belongings. They were leaving Rexford, Montana and moving to Coal County, Oklahoma.

They had been to church at Ora Millers the day before for the last time before moving away. There had been lots of

Mart and Susan's new house. After living in the shop for three years it was very nice to live in a house again.

men to help in loading the shanty and women to help Susan with washing laundry for the last time and last-minute packing.

Their sale had been on April 20, and most of their farm equipment and all the horses except two were sold at the sale. Mart's mother, brother Atlee and wife Drusilla and sons Daniel and Reuben, brother Abe and wife Anna, and sister Kathy and four children had arrived at Whitefish, Montana two days before the sale. Now they were going back home except Atlees and two boys and Mother would travel by train to Mexico for Atlee's checkup at the clinic. Mart and Susan and the boys would be traveling with them to Mexico.

On April 22 was the last day on the West Kootenai for Marts. After the shanty was loaded and all packing was done, Marts and Atlees and Mother went to Roman Schla-

This is the back view of the house at Marts. The Bewick's wren used to have its nest somewhere in the back yard every summer.

This is the shop as it looks today. Here Mart and Susan and the two boys made their home for three years. The old hackberry tree is still standing, but you can see where a storm broke one of the main branches off. Susan was in the shop at the time and saw it happen.

bachs for supper yet, then they all left from there to Libby to board the train at 10:30 p.m. No one of the family was going with the semi. Just the two dogs, Herbie the Border collie and Penny the Pomeranian who was old and blind.

The next morning, on April 23, they woke up around the Moses Lake area in Washington. Lots of orchards blooming and beautiful flowers all around. Then went through the mountains again and saw snow too. Quite a contrast. Traveled on to Seattle; lots of nice farmland after leaving Seattle. Oregon had green, green pastures and nice farms.

On April 24, Marts and the others woke up in California. The train was a nice way to travel. A beautiful sunrise

This is a view from Ben B. Troyers' lane looking out over their pasture field with their horses grazing. Marts' house and shop are in the background.

promised a beautiful day and they traveled on to Sacramento, San Francisco, Los Angeles, and finally San Diego where a Delmar taxi van picked them all up at the train depot.

On April 25, was Marts' first day in Mexico. They ate breakfast at El Yogurt. In the forenoon Mart went with Atlee to the hospital. In the afternoon they all went downtown to Tiawana marketplace on the streets. Ate supper by the ocean.

On April 26, the women did laundry in the forenoon. We all had a chicken dinner at Atlees' hut in p.m. around 3:00. The other Amish couples that were at the clinic at that time were there too. They were Ivan Rabers of Holmesville, Ohio, Jr. Hershbergers of Danville, Ohio, and Joas Lambrights of Orange County, Indiana.

Marts and the boys left Atlees' hut at 4:00 p.m. and took a

taxi to the trolley. Then by trolley to San Diego. There they boarded the train to Los Angeles.

On April 27, Marts and the boys boarded the Sunset Limited around midnight and traveled through Arizona and New Mexico. Saw lots of cactus.

April 28, traveled through Texas. Such a big state! Ate breakfast at San Antonio and arrived in Dallas at 5:28 in evening. Their train ride was now over. They slept in a motel that night and the next morning on April 29, at 7:00 they boarded the bus for Atoka, Oklahoma. They were almost there at last. They arrived in Atoka that same forenoon at 10:30 where Susan's sister Esta was waiting with a driver. They were finally at the end of their journey.

Marts went to Vernon and Esta's house to stay until the truck arrived with their belongings and the dogs. The semi

Marts' barn as it looks today. This was the part where the horse stalls were.

had several breakdowns on the way and their stay at Vernons was quite a bit longer than they had planned. But eventually the semi did arrive and Mart and Susan and the two boys moved on the farm in the new shop building Mart had built on his previous trip to Oklahoma in March.

The first three years on the farm were busy ones with a dairy. Milking cows kept Mart and Susan and the boys on a prompt schedule. Everything seemed to be scheduled around milking time. Then when the drought came in 1988, the Hochstetlers decided to sell the dairy cows and get beef cattle or stocker cattle. Usually stocker cattle are somewhere between weaning age and two years of age. Their rations are usually based on forages. They graze both winter pastures and summer pastures.

Clean-tilled mixtures of rye and wheat or oats and rye grass are usually planted for grazing only. Soil preparations and soil management are important factors in planting winter pastures. The weather in Oklahoma has some extremes and the soil varies even on the same farm. Mart had to get the soil tested and apply fertilizer and lime as needed.

A non-Amish neighbor was hired to prepare the soil and break up the hard crust. A sufficient method is the use of a tandem disc and harrow. A chisel plow can also be used to break up compacted soil layers.

Mart and Susan started building their new house in the fall of 1987. After living in the shop for three years they moved into the new house in the spring of 1988. It wasn't all finished, but enough that they could live in it. It was so nice to live in a house again.

They lived in the new house almost four years, then they decided to move to West Union, Ohio. On the morning of December 2, 1991, amidst an Oklahoma ice storm, they started off, after several hours of delay, for their new home in West Union, Ohio. The red shanty was once again loaded with their belongings. Steven and Edwin traveled with the semi hauling the red shanty, and Martin and Susan traveled with the big U-Haul moving truck, not knowing what the future would hold, but knowing who holds the future.

Susan is a daughter to Elmer, #24-A, and a sister to Esta, #17.

Family #24-A—Elmer Troyers

Elmer M. Troyer was born February 22, 1917, to Mose and Elizabeth (Miller) Troyer. He was married to Katie D. (Schlabach) Troyer. She was a daughter of Daniel and Amanda (Yoder) Schlabach of Mt. Hope, Ohio.

Children

Edwin Daniel	August 28, 1945
#24. Susan Irene	June 23, 1947
Elizabeth Mae	February 4, 1950
Mary Ellen	June 5, 1951
#17. Esta	December 5, 1952

Elmer spent a lot of time in California in the High Sierra Mountains while in CPS (Civilian Public Service) camp. He was on the north fork of the San Joaquin River, on the lookout towers to watch for forest fires.

While there he turned out vases and small items out of alabaster rock in his spare time when not on duty.

Elmer and Katie moved to Winesburg, Ohio after his service and from there to west of Holmesville, Ohio, renting a farm from Melvin B. Miller. In the fall of 1951, they bought an eighty-acre farm several miles from Melvins' farm and moved there yet that fall. Here they lived until 1965, when they sold the farm and moved to Florida for one whole year for Elmer's health. The warmer winters agreed with him. They moved to the Apple Creek area and rented at three different places until they moved to the Holmesville area again but not in the same church district as before. From here they moved to the New Bedford area. While living here Katie was diagnosed with lymphoma cancer and four years later she died in Oklahoma after moving there to Martin and Susan's farm in May of 1985. She passed away on July 17, 1985, first burial in Clarita Amish cemetery. Elmer and Katie spent most of their winters in Florida.

Elmer went back to Ohio to visit family after Katie's funeral and came back to Oklahoma during the summers and went to Florida during the winters. He bought Vernon and

This is the house in Clarita that Elmer Troyer (Florida Dawdy) bought from Vernons. Vernon was a gardener and planted hedges, shrubbery, and flowers. Esta took good care of them. They built a low fence along the hedge roses.

Esta's place in Clarita and later sold it to Daniel C. Masts.

Elmer married the second time on July 4, 1990, to Barbara Kay Hochstetler at Topeka, Indiana. She was born on November 3, 1947, to Daniel A. and Katie (Eash) Hochstetler. Dan was the founder of D. A. Hochstetler and Sons of Topeka, Indiana.

After the wedding Elmer and Barbara moved to Florida and lived there for ten years. In the year 2000 they sold their house in Florida and came to live in West Union, Ohio where Martin and Susan now lived. During the winter they still go to Florida on the Pioneer Trails bus and rent an apartment in Pine Craft area of Sarasota.

At the time of this writing Elmer is eighty-six years old and the only one of his family still living.

Family #25—Allen & Mary Yoder

Allen Ray Yoder was born on January 27, 1963, to Nelson and Ida (Miller) Yoder of Chouteau, Oklahoma. He married Mary Hershberger on April 17, 1986. She was born September 10, 1964, daughter of Melvin and Mattie (Troyer) Hershberger of Coalgate, Oklahoma (Clarita settlement).

Children

Esther	March 14, 1987
Nelson Jay	September 26, 1989
Melvin Lee	August 12, 1991
Martha Ann	May 12, 1993
Rachel Sue	July 4, 1996
Mervin Dean	May 25, 1998

Allen and Mary lived on the former Menno Yoder place after their wedding and milked cows and raised calves. Later they moved to a 160-acre place south of Herman Yoders that Allen's dad, Nelson Yoder, helped them buy. They lived eight years on that place and had beef cows. Allen started working for John Henry Miller's crew, building steel structure buildings and still works there. In November of 2001, Ervin Yoders wanted to sell their place which joins Allens' farm. Ervin Yoders had bought their place from Herman Yoder. Herman had bought two parcels from Scott Millican.

Allen has seventeen beehives he takes care of. They sell honey at Melvin Hershbergers' country store (Mary's parents). They also sell a lot of honey at the annual school auction.

Mary bakes pies every week for the store. During the summer she cans enough pickles to supply the store for one whole year. She also makes peach jam to sell. She also quilts

Allen and Mary Yoder's house. This is the house Ervin Yoders built. Allens bought Ervins' place when they moved away.

The dairy barn at Allens that Ervins built. Allens use it for dog kennels to raise Jack Russel puppies.

Allens also raise calves. Their children are a big help on the farm.

Here is where Allens lived before buying Ervins' place. They still own this place. The two places are side by side. They still have chores to do here too.

for the school auction.

Mary also takes care of the whelping house where they have thirty-five Jack Russel females. So I guess they have gone to the dogs too. But in a good way. They also turned the milk barn into dog kennels, and the milk house for the whelping house. Their oldest children are good helpers.

Allen is a brother to Lydia Anne, #26. Mary is a daughter to Melvins, #7, and a sister to Abe, #26, and Ada, #28.

Family #26—Abe & Lydia Hershberger

Abe Hershberger was born February 19, 1966, to Melvin and Mattie (Troyer) Hershberger of Coalgate, Oklahoma. He married Lydia Anne Yoder on October 9, 1986, at Chouteau, Oklahoma. She was born on March 10, 1964, to Nelson and Ida (Miller) Yoder of Chouteau.

Abe and Lydia's dairy barn. The dog feels right at home by
the barn.

Children

Jacob	May 1, 1988 *(premature—3 lbs. 1oz.)*
Ida Mae	December 13, 1989
Daniel Ray	February 1, 1998
Jonathan	March 1, 2001

Abes moved to the south end of the Clarita settlement
after their wedding to the 130-acre farm that used to be
the Atlee Stutzman farm. They have a dairy and milk cows.
They have an average of fifty cows they milk twice a day.
Their milk goes to Lone Star Milk Producers Co-op—Grade
A—in Sulphur Springs, Texas.

Lydia baked chiffon cakes and banana bread for Melvin
Hershbergers' country store for eleven years. They make
apple butter once a year in the fall for the store too. They
and Allens help each other with that project.

Abes' farm at a distance. The roads are not winding in the Clarita area. Although some of the land is slightly rolling, the roads are pretty well straight except for highway 48.

The new house Abe and Lydia built after living in a trailer for many years.

Abes get the newborn goats (males) from Nathan Stutzmans and raise them until they are ready for market.

Abe and Lydia Anne lived in a trailer until they got their new house built.

Abe is a son to Melvins, #7, a brother to Mary, #25, and Ada, #28. Lydia Anne is a sister to Allen, #25.

Family #27—Edward & Ruby Yoder

Edward E. Yoder was born on October 11, 1965, to Elmer D. and Pauline (Hebeggar) Yoder of Bloomfield, Iowa. He married April 30, 1987, to Ruby Fern Mast, a daughter to Daniel C. and Verna (Mast) Mast of Coalgate, Oklahoma. She was born March 20, 1966.

Children

Wayne	August 10, 1988

Edward was the school teacher at Elm Creek School. He

The old orchard on the old place where Dan Masts lived was across the drive from Edward and Ruby's trailer.

also worked for Yoder Construction. They lived in a trailer at Dan Masts (Ruby's parents).

Edward and Ruby with baby Wayne moved to Ludington, Michigan on April 23, 1990.

Ruby is a daughter to Daniels, #6.

Family #28—Freeman & Ada Yoder

Freeman Ray Yoder of Chouteau, Oklahoma was born July 31, 1965, to Emanuel and Minnie (Gingerich) Yoder. He married Ada Hershberger on October 15, 1987. She was born November 12, 1960, to Melvin and Mattie (Troyer) Hershberger of Coalgate, Oklahoma.

Freemans moved to Melvin Hershbergers in a trailer after the wedding. Freeman worked for Yoder Construction. In the evenings and on Saturdays he worked in his buggy shop. He bought Vernon Millers' inventory when they

This is the log house that Ora Hochstetlers built, and where Freeman and Ada Yoder now live.

Freemans' barn from the road.

moved back to Ohio.

Ada baked bread, cinnamon rolls, and fruitcakes for Melvins' country store. They lived there at Melvins in the trailer for seven years.

In the fall of 1994, Freemans moved to the Ora Hochstetler farm and started a dairy after Oras moved away. Freemans bought Ben J. Troyers' dairy cows when Bens moved to Crab Orchard, Kentucky. They also bought heifers from Freeman's dad and other private dairies.

Freeman moved his buggy shop business along to the new farm. The last two years he also has the wheel repair business which he got from Allen Yoder.

In 2001, Freeman and Ada quit milking and he is now working for John Henry Miller's crew since last fall. They raise Holstein heifers which they buy from dairies in Texas as calves and raise them to sell as springers. They are also starting a beef herd.

Ada a is daughter of Melvins, #7, a sister to Abe, #26, and

A close-up of the dairy barn at Freemans, also built by Ora Hochstetlers.

Mary, #25.

Family #29   Cristie & Mary Miller

Cristie Miller was born May 31, 1965, to Albert C. and Fannie (Kuhns) Miller of Nappanee, Indiana. He married Mary Yoder on October 20, 1988 at Chouteau, Oklahoma. She was born to Nelson and Ida (Miller) Yoder of Chouteau on January 10, 1970.

Cristie and Mary moved to Clarita, Oklahoma soon after their wedding to the property where Vernon Millers used to live, which Elmer Troyer then bought from Vernons and rented out. Daniel C. Masts bought it from Elmer.

Cristie and Mary lived in Clarita from October 25, 1988, to May 19, 1989, then they moved back to Chouteau. They helped on the home farm at Nelsons, then later moved to Mt. Vernon, Missouri. They now have two little boys.

Family #30—Ora & Florence Hochstetler

Ora J. Hochstetler, born March 10, 1950, to Joe N. and Gertrude (Mast) Hochstetler of Jamesport, Missouri. He married Florence Kramer on November 16, 1972.

She was born August 23, 1949, to Ralph W. and Amanda (Yutzy) Kramer of Jamesport, Missouri.

Ora and Florence moved to Coal County, Oklahoma from Jamesport, Missouri on December 14, 1988.

They lived on the Mel Troyer place until they had built their dairy barn on the land they bought. They moved a trailer in to live in and started milking cows in the new barn.

They eventually built a new log home. Ora did a lot of the building himself, with occasional help from Herman Stutzmans' boys.

Ora bought ten of Mart Hochstetlers' cows when Marts

Ora Hochstetlers' barn from the road.

sold their dairy cows. But eventually he changed his dairy herd over from Holsteins to Jerseys.

Oras moved back to Jamesport, Missouri on September 6, 1994, and at the time of this writing they are living at Redding, Iowa.

Florence's parents, Ralph Kramers, used to live in Plain City, Ohio before moving to Jamesport, Missouri.

Florence is a sister to Edna, #35.

Family #31—Joe & Mary Mast

Joe L. Mast, born March 1, 1949, to Henry and Mary (Hochstetler) Mast of Jamesport, Missouri. He married Mary Bontrager on May 4, 1972. She was born February 5, 1951, to Levi and Irene (Yoder) Bontrager of Hardwood, Texas. (Later moved to Clare, Michigan.)

Children

	Arlene	April 20, 1973
#38.	Irene	February 24, 1975
	Kathryn	June 17, 1978
	Carol	December 22, 1980
	Robert	August 4, 1982
	Irma	July 26, 1990

Joe and Mary moved to Coal County, Oklahoma from Jamesport, Missouri on February 23, 1989.

Joe was an experienced blacksmith and a good one. He shoed horses on every weekday but Thursdays, in the barn there on the property they bought east of highway 48 across from the Mel Troyer place.

The two oldest girls, Arlene and Irene, milked cows for Curtis Nelson on his dairy not far from Joes. They also did some baby-sitting.

Joes built a large washhouse beside their house and this added a few bedrooms for the girls plus a bath and a nice big room to take church in.

On Thursdays, when Joe didn't shoe horses at home, he went out elsewhere to shoe horses. But eventually that day was spent hunting wild hogs with a group of men who were experienced hog hunters. They took dogs and caught the wild hogs after tranquilizing them, then loaded them up in a trailer and took them to ranches where they brought hunters in to shoot them. The dogs they took along on these hunts were often chewed up by the wild hogs. The men sometimes sewed them up or used super glue to fix the tears.

Joes had a fabric store which Mary took care of. They also carried Coleman parts, shoes, and hats.

Joe and Mary Mast's house. He was the community blacksmith. The washhouse in the back was built for church services and extra bedrooms and a bath.

Joes moved to Crab Orchard, Kentucky on July 31, 1997. They are parents to Irene, #38.

Family #32—Robert & Esther Miller

Robert Lynn Miller, born September 17, 1964, to Raymond E. and Elsie (Hostetler) Miller. He married Esther Hershberger on November 26, 1987. She was born February 25, 1969, to Mark and Mary (Mast) Hershberger from Kalona, Iowa.

Children

Jeffrey Lee	July 24, 1988
Kathy Jo	January 8, 1990
Carrie Ann	July 30, 1991
Edwin Ray	December 28, 1993
Ruth Ellen	October 4, 1995

Robert and Esther's new house has a wraparound porch and spacious rooms inside.

Roberts' shop as seen from the house. They lived in part of the shop until their house was built.

Benjamin Mark	October 18, 1997
Sara Jean	July 29, 2002
Naomi Sue	July 5, 2003

Robert and Esther moved to Coal County, Oklahoma from Stephenville, Texas on September 26, 1989. At first they moved to the old house where his grandparents, #8, used to live.

Roberts then bought sixty acres from Loyal Brewer on the east side of highway 48 in about the middle of the community. They built a shop first and fixed one end to move into.

Robert did carpenter work with Norman Miller the first two years, and they also had a truck patch where they grew a variety of vegetables to sell. He then started making lawn furniture in his new shop and now also makes cabinets.

Roberts built a big new house, with Norman helping with the work. They live in the new house about one year now at the time of this writing. They have nice big rooms which are needed for their growing family.

They have a nice young orchard and the place is groomed and pruned up real nicely. They have a good-sized greenhouse and sell bedding plants and flowers to the public.

Robert is a son of Raymonds, #1, a brother to Edwin, #40, Lovina, #41, John Henry, #43, Reuben, #45, and Cindy, #46.

Family #33—Harvey & Wilma Troyer

Harvey M. Troyer was born December 3, 1949, to Melvin and Lizzie Ann (Farmwald) Troyer of Garnett, Kansas. He married Wilma Marie Yoder on September 24, 1970. She was born June 10, 1952, to Ira J. and Ida (Miller) Yoder of Garnett.

Children

Darrel Glen	August 18, 1971	
David Leon	June 16, 1973 - died June 24, 1983	
#45. Nancy Renee	July 27, 1975	
Dean Lavon	June 13, 1978	
DeWayne Lee	May 26, 1980	
Lisa Fern	September 16, 1983	
Floyd Ray	July 7, 1986	

Harvey and Wilma moved to Coal County, Oklahoma from Sulphur Springs, Texas on June 3, 1991. They had moved to Texas from Garnett, Kansas. They moved to the north end of the settlement across highway 48 from Norman Millers and just north of Elmer Yoders. They first moved into Perry Summy's trailer until their shop was built. They

The big shop that Harvey and Wilma built. Their living quarters were on the left side with their barn on the right.

built a large shop of steel structures and fixed the one end up to move into. They had exotic fowl and Harvey and the boys worked for Yoder Construction. Harvey and the boys had a large cement job in Texas. Some of the other men in the community went along too.

Four years later, on July 13, 1995, Harveys moved to Mt. Vernon, Missouri and built a large house. Harvey and the boys did a lot of the work themselves. Then several years later Harvey was diagnosed with cancer and he suffered several years (with some good days too). He passed away on August 26, 2001.

The children are all married now except Lisa and Floyd. Wilma has many lonely days. She sent in the following poem.

Daddy Dear

Today's your birthday, Daddy Dear,

I think of you each hour…
Oh, how I wish to see your face,
To release my heart of sorrow.
The days seem long, oh Daddy Dear,
Since you have left my side.
I wish you'd walk back in the door,
With me, once more confide.

Our family—oh Daddy Dear,
Has grown six by two…
A precious little grandchild,
Has joined the lively crew.
A baby girl—oh, what a surprise…
After four little boys in a row.
Oh, how I wish to hold them near,
And keep them from all woe.

Oh Daddy Dear, you're missed so much!
Tho we wouldn't wish you back…
Into this world of greed and hate,
And so many evil acts.
With Christmas season coming up,
A spot will empty be…
No one can ever fill that spot—
No one, Daddy Dear, but thee.

We trust you're up in Heaven now,
In Jesus' loving arms…
Oh, how we'd like to join you,
Up there away from harm!
It seems so hard to understand,

The will of God each day...
But if we only trust in Him.
He'll gently lead the way!

"Saviour, like a shepherd lead us,
Much we need Thy tenderest care;
In thy pleasant pastures feed us,
For our use Thy folds prepare...
"Blessed Jesus, Blessed Jesus...
Hear, oh, hear us when we pray..."

Family #34—Perry & Alma Summy

Perry Summy was born January 12, 1955, to Pete and Effie (Hochstetler) Summy of Somerset County, Pennsylvania. He married Alma Yoder on August 26, 1976. She was born

Perry Summys built this barn and moved a trailer in to live in.
The trailer is not there anymore.

November 19, 1957, to Wilmer and Elizabeth (Slabaugh) Yoder of Somerset County.

Perry and Alma moved to Coal County, Oklahoma from Sulphur Springs, Texas on July 1, 1991. They lived at the north end too, just up the road from Harvey Troyers and Elmer Yoders and not far from Mart Hochstetlers. They bought ten acres from Evertt Krebs. Their land joins Harveys'.

Perry worked for Yoder Construction and Alma pieced quilts and quilted. They built a small barn and moved a trailer in to live in.

Perrys moved to Mt. Vernon, Missouri a few months before Harveys did. Their moving date was May 19, 1995.

Alma passed away on January 22, 2000 in Mt. Vernon. She also died from cancer. Perry remarried and is living in Humansville, Missouri.

Family #35—Joe & Edna Petersheim

Joseph J. Petersheim was born August 23, 1950, to Joe and Mattie (Yoder) Petersheim of Haven, Kansas. He married Edna Ellen Kramer on October 30, 1975. She was born January 20, 1951, to Ralph W. and Amanda (Yutzy) Kramer of Jamesport, Missouri (formerly of Plain City, Ohio).

Joe and Edna moved from Haven, Kansas to Coal County, Oklahoma on February 4, 1992.

Children

Joseph Leroy	August 31, 1976
Loretta Kay	November 3, 1978
Lillian Sue	September 19, 1980
Johnny Ray	October 24, 1982
David Lavon	August 27, 1987
Donna Marie	August 24, 1987
Abe Matthew	April 11, 1990

Joe and Edna lived here on the Robinson place.

Joes built a dairy barn on their farm and milked cows. This is a view from the road.

Joe was ordained a deacon in the Clarita church April 20, 1996. He was the only deacon the Clarita church ever had. Joes started up a dairy and milked cows. He did carpenter work part-time. They bought the Mel Troyer place first and lived there for three years and had a dairy. Then Joes bought the Robinson place from Herman Yoders and moved there. They had a dairy there and lived there for two years.

On January 21, 1997, Joes moved to Charlotte, Michigan and still live there at the time of this writing.

Joe is a brother to Dorothy, #22. Edna is a sister to Florence, #30.

Family #36—Jonas & Ruth Miller

Jonas L. Miller was born August 3, 1938, to Levi M. and Mattie (Byler) Miller of Crawford County, Pennsylvania. He married Ruth J. Kauffman on September 26, 1958. She was born December 14, 1940, to Joe C. and Lizzie (Byler) Kauffman of Geauga County, Ohio.

Jonas and Ruth lived in Indiana after their marriage. Later they moved to Texas to work on a dairy farm. They moved to Coal County, Oklahoma on July 24, 1992, from Stephenville, Texas. They lived in Mart Hochstetlers' house until Davy Yoders moved in from Haven, Kansas. Davys had bought part of Mart and Susan's place. They didn't move right away, so Jonas and Ruth rented it.

Jonas helped his son Mel Ray in his cabinet shop. The cabinet shop was just down the road a ways. They could easily walk back and forth.

Children

#18. Mel Ray	May 6, 1959
Erma Jane	November 3, 1960
Stillborn girl	November 24, 1961
Esther-Stillborn	July 12, 1962

Jonas and Ruth Miller rented this house in Clarita after Davy
Yoder moved into the Mart Hochstetler house where they had
rented first.

Stillborn boy　　　January 29, 1964

After Davy Yoders moved in, Jonas and Ruth moved to
Clarita and rented a house there. Jonas still worked for Mel
Ray. He took the buggy to work then or hitchhiked a way.
He worked some for Elmer Yoder's construction crew when
Mel Ray's business was slow.

Jonas and Ruth moved back to Stephenville, Texas on
April 11, 1994, and later moved to Indiana again.

Jonas and Ruth are parents to Mel Ray, #18.

Family #37—David & Heidi Stutzman

David Leon Stutzman was born April 27, 1969 to Herman N. and Dorothy (Petersheim) Stutzman from Coalgate, Oklahoma. He married Heidi Yoder on September 17,

David and Heidi lived and worked on the Janet Milligan ranch.

1992. She was born on July 17, 1971, to Herman Ray and Ida (Yoder) Yoder of Coalgate, Oklahoma.

Children

Sharon Ann	August 12, 199
Jonathan Tobias	December 19, 1994
Freeman David	July 19, 1997
Matthew Aaron	April 18, 1999
Marlin Wayne	May 13, 2002

David and Heidi moved to the Janet Milligan Ranch after their wedding. They lived and worked on the ranch for six years until they moved to Kalona, Iowa on February 2, 1998. David helped milk at Jacobs in the mornings on the Herman Yoder farm.

David is a son to Herman Stutzmans, #22 and brother to Jacob, #42. Heidi is a daughter of Herman Yoders, #19 and sister to Lori, #42.

Family #38—Andrew & Irene Miller

Andrew Miller was born May 28, 1972, to Andy A. and Mary D. (Yoder) Miller of Clarita, Oklahoma. He married Irene Mast on December 3, 1992. She was born February 24, 1975 to Joe L. and Mary (Bontrager) Mast of Clarita, Oklahoma.

Children

Robert Allen	May 5, 1993
Edwin Lee	July 19, 1994
Richard Ray	May 10, 1997
Darvin Wayne	January 28, 2000

Andrew and Irene bought a house in Clarita that had belonged to Babe Ray's son. They lived there from December

Andrew and Irene lived in this trailer at Melvin Hershbergers, before moving to West Union, Ohio.

1992 to August 1993. They sold the house to Jeff Aubury and went to Texas to work for Larry Mitchell on his dairy in Sulphur Springs. They worked there for one year, then moved back to Clarita and rented the Mel Troyer place for one year. While living there Andrew worked for Mel Ray Miller in his cabinet shop, and also helped Gus Martin on his ranch. From the Troyer place they moved to Melvin Hershbergers in the trailer that Freeman and Ada used to live in. Here Andrew worked for John Henry Miller building large hog barns.

They moved to West Union, Ohio in August of 1997. Andrew is a son of Andys, #23. Irene is a daughter of Joes, #31.

Family #39—Davy & Carol Yoder

David Lee Yoder was born July 13, 1962, to David T. and Sylvia (Miller) Yoder of Garnett, Kansas. He married Carol Ann Eash on October 16, 1987. She was born November 6, 1966, to Ervin and Alice (Yoder) Eash of Haven, Kansas.

Davy and Carol moved to Coal County, Oklahoma on April 16, 1993. They bought the former Mart Hochstetler place. (Fifteen to twenty acres and the buildings.)

Children

Steven Duane	August 12, 1988
Marvin Davon	October 20, 1990
Miriam Renae	August 27, 1992
Samuel Lee	May 13, 1994

Davy worked for Elmer Yoder's construction crew. They lived in the Clarita settlement two years, then decided to move back to Kansas.

Davy and Carol Yoder lived here on the former Mart Hochstetler place for two years until they moved back to Kansas.

A view of Davy and Carol's house from the road.

Family #40—Edwin & Esther Miller

Edwin Miller was born November 22, 1965, to Raymond E. and Elsie (Hostetler) Miller. He married on May 31, 1990, to Esther Troyer. She was born on April 29, 1969, to Ben B. and Emma (Mast) Troyer.

Edwin and Esther were married in Clarita. Although Ben and Emma were still working in Texas, they came to their farm in Coal County to get ready for the wedding there. The wedding church was in Vernon Millers' new shop, just across the road and southeast a little from Bens' place.

Edwin and Esther returned to Stephenville, Texas after the wedding. They moved back to Coal County, Oklahoma July 1, 1993, after working on a dairy three years.

Children

Karen Sue	June 23, 1991
Vernon Lee	August 13, 1993
Laura Beth	August 4, 1996
Lucinda Marie	November 15, 1998
Mary Lou	November 16, 1999
Barbara Ann	September 2, 2001
Emma Jean	January 1, 2004

Edwins lived at Levi and Lovina's place until they built a new house of their own on the place where Edwin's grandparents had lived (Ben Hostetlers, #8). Norman Miller was the main carpenter to build the house.

Edwin did carpenter work part-time and worked for Gus Martin part-time on his ranch, until they started a full-time dairy. They now milk around forty cows (Holsteins) and have a busy schedule. They also raise Bernice Mountain dogs and have some pecan trees which are harvested each

Edwin and Esther's new house—front view. The old house where Ben and Alma Hostetler used to live is no longer there.

Edwins' dairy barn. They are full-time dairy farmers.

fall.

Edwins enjoy the purple martins and have interest in housing them as do most of the Amish in the community.

Edwins lease some hay fields for enough hay for their dairy.

Edwin is a son of Raymonds, #1, brother to Robert, #32, Lovina, #41, John Henry, #43, Reuben, #45, and Cindy, #46. Esther is a daughter of Bens, #11, and sister to Levi, #41, Daniel, #47, and John, #48.

Family #41—Levi & Lovina Troyer

Levi Troyer was born July 6, 1967, to Ben B. and Emma (Mast) Troyer. He married June 28, 1986, to Lovina Miller. She was born October 2, 1968, to Raymond E. and Elsie (Hostetler) Miller.

Bens and Raymonds both still lived and worked in Dublin, Texas at the time of the wedding, so the wedding was in Texas, and Levi and Lovina stayed there to work seven more years.

Levi and Lovina moved back to Coal County, Oklahoma on July 30, 1993. They had bought the former Menno E. Yoder farm.

Children

Leanna	October 20, 1986
Junior	October 1, 1988
Kristine	May 20, 1992
Michael John	May 14, 1995
Elsie Marie	October 1, 1996 - Died June 17, 1999
Norman Lee	December 1, 1998

Levis have a large pecan grove on their farm. They had

Levi and Lovina's house. They are in the process of putting on new vinyl siding and a new deck.

a dairy there and milked cows until the last couple years they raised dogs too instead of milking. They raise Bernice Mountain dogs, Jack Russels, and Pugs. More Pugs than Jack Russels. A broker comes around and picks out what he wants and then takes them to Atoka and from there to Missouri, and then they go all over the country to different pet shops. The Bernice Mountain females are usually sold privately, and can bring as much as $1500.00. An awesome sum for a dog or puppy.

Leanna and Junior are a big help at home for Lovina. She raises dogs while Levi works for John Henry's crew (Lovina's brother).

In the fall Bobby Woods usually harvests their pecan grove. But the last year O.N. Riley did.

Little Elsie Marie died in a farm accident at home and is

buried in the Clarita Amish cemetery at Melvin Hershberg-ers.

Levi is a son to Bens, #11, and a brother to #40, #47, and #48. Lovina is a daughter to Raymonds, #1, sister to Robert, #32, Edwin, #40, John Henry, #43, Reuben, #45, and Cindy, #46.

Family #42—Jacob & Lori Stutzman

Jacob Wayne Stutzman was born July 12, 1970, to Herman and Dorothy (Petersheim) Stutzman. He married Lori Ann Yoder on April 6, 1994. She was born April 6, 1973, to Herman and Ida Yoder.

Both Jacob and Lori's parents lived in Coal County at the time of the wedding.

Jacobs moved to the Mel Troyer place after the wedding and lived there until August 1994, when Lori's parents (Herman Yoders) moved to Kalona, Iowa. Then Jacob and Lori moved over on Hermans' farm and took over the dairy. They lived there and milked cows and farmed until December 10, 1998, when they also moved to Kalona, Iowa. Lori had some health problems and after Davids had moved in February it was quite lonely for Lori, being the only one left of her family.

Children

Samuel Glenn	April 11, 1995
Karen Marie	February 2, 1997
Ruth Ann	October 3, 2000
Steven Jacob	March 5, 2003

Jacobs lived in Stringtown in the Kalona area. He worked in a salvage store (Bent and Dent) and Davids lived on Jacobs' place. Lori's health is better now and in February of

Jacobs lived on the Herman Yoder farm and farmed—had
a dairy.

2003, Jacobs moved to their own place. Herman Stutzmans
came from Coal County, Oklahoma to help them move. Davids also moved on a place of their own. It was a cold February day. So both Jacobs and Davids are settled in Kalona
now and after moving was over the men's parents went back
to their home in Clarita, Oklahoma where the winters are
milder.

Jacob is a son of Hermans, #22, brother to #37.

Family #43—John Henry & Anna Marie Miller

John Henry Miller was born March 16, 1972, to Raymond
E. and Elsie (Hostetler) Miller. He married Anna Marie Yoder on September 15, 1994. She was born June 10, 1973, to
Alva M. and Susan (Borntrager) Yoder of Chouteau, Oklahoma.

After the wedding in Chouteau, John Henry and Anna Marie moved to Coal County. He bought land near Olney, and built a shop building which they fixed up at the one end for living quarters.

John Henry has a large construction crew. At first he built large hog barns and now builds Steel Structure buildings. He also has a dairy. His wife Anna Marie was the milkmaid until the twins were born, then she was busy tending babies. So John Henry quit the crew for awhile, but is back on the job again. They shut the dairy down for now but have plans of starting up again someday. He should have lots of help when their boys grow up.

Children
>Raymond Devon June 11, 1995
>Darrel Wayne   August 13, 1997

John Henry Millers' new house. They lived in the shop before the house was built. Shop not shown.

John Henrys' dairy barn.

Jay Dean	June 14, 1999
John Dale	June 14, 1999
Aaron Lee	September 21, 2002

John Henry is a son to Raymonds, #1, a brother to Robert, #32, Edwin, #40, Lovina, #41, Reuben, #45, and Cindy, #46.

Family #44—Ervin & Katie Mae Yoder

Ervin J. Yoder was born on March 5, 1959, to John H. and Ada Mae (Miller) Yoder of Guthrie, Kentucky (formerly of Jamesport, Missouri). He married Katie Mae Schrock on May 7, 1980. She was born August 9, 1959, to Eli M. and Verna (Beachy) Schrock of Chouteau (formerly of Jamesport, Missouri).

Ervin and Katie Mae moved to Coal County, Oklahoma

on January 3, 1995, from Guthrie Kentucky. It was after the decision was made to allow tractor farming. In 1994, after much counseling in the church, this decision was made. However, quite a few were opposed to this and for other reasons too, about ten families moved out of Coal County in the fall of 1994 and spring of 1995.

But Ervin and Katie Mae decided to move in and bought the Scott Millican place from Herman Yoder. They pushed over the old house and built a new one. They also built a new dairy barn and had a dairy. They got Jersey cows to milk but sold them later and got Holsteins.

Ervin did some carpenter work too. He also put up a shop and they built storage barns and small cabins.

Children

      Vernon Dale   October 18, 1981

Ervin and Katie Mae Yoder built this house and lived here until they moved to Crab Orchard, Kentucky.

The dairy barn Ervins built. They milked Jerseys at first and later sold them and got Holsteins.

Leah Irene	March 4, 1983
Frieda Marie	January 29, 1985
Lovina Lynn	October 19, 1986
Wayne Edward	January 4, 1989
Mary Kaylene	April 16, 1991
Matthew Ray	November 23, 1999
Aaron Jay	March 11, 2002

Ervin was ordained minister in the Clarita church on September 17, 1995.

Ervins moved to Crab Orchard, Kentucky on November 5, 2001.

Family #45—Reuben & Nancy Miller

Reuben Miller was born November 1, 1973, to Raymond E. and Elsie (Hostetler) Miller from Coalgate, Oklahoma.

He married Nancy Renee Troyer on April 6, 1995. She was born July 27, 1975, to Harvey M. and Wilma (Yoder) Troyer of Coalgate (formerly of Garnett, Kansas).

After the wedding Reuben and Nancy moved in a trailer on the Larry Cribbs dairy farm. They worked for Larry on the dairy for one year.

Their first child, Julianna Marie, was born here on February 2, 1996. They moved to Mt. Vernon, Missouri on April 27, 1996, and still live there at the time of this writing. Jeremy and Christopher were born at Mt. Vernon, Missouri.

Nancy wrote the following poem after her father, Harvey, passed away from cancer while they lived in Mt. Vernon, Missouri, August 26, 2001. He was actually at Garnett, Kansas when he died.

Reuben is a son of Raymonds, #1. Nancy is a daughter of Harveys, #33.

Daddy Dear Good-bye
What are we going to do now, the future looks so dim,
We can only trust in him, we will miss you dearly
But that's okay daddy dear, because daddy dear we know,
That your pain is over, and that you're at home
Where we have longed to be.

Oh daddy dear we know it was hard,
To leave us all here, how wonderful it would've been,
If we could've all gone with you,
Hand in hand together into this promised land.

Oh daddy dear what could we do for mom,

We can hold her close and comfort her here
And daddy dear you know,
We could never take the place of you daddy dear,
We want to do what we can with Jesus to help us
And comfort our mama dear.

Oh daddy dear mom will miss you forever,
At night when she lies down and reaches for you,
So please daddy dear tell Jesus to be there,
Although mom was sometimes weary of taking care of
you,
Those times will always be precious to her.

Oh daddy dear how deeply we care,
For dear brother Floyd,
Things will now change for him,
He will now be mom's right hand,
What a big responsibility for such a young man.
We will always be there to help him along,
The best we can, he now has no one
To call daddy dear,
So please daddy dear tell Jesus to be there.

Oh daddy dear for Lisa we care,
For mama will need her like never before,
Wasn't Lisa just hoping that you would be there,
On that wonderful day, when she would show every-
one,
That she will live for Jesus,
So please daddy dear tell Jesus to be there.

Oh daddy dear for brother DeWayne,

We also feel so much the day that he takes,
Sister Marilyn to be his wife,
We had so much hope that on their special day,
That you could be there to bless their wedded life,
But daddy we know that your wonderful spirit,
Will let them know that you are there,
So daddy dear tell Jesus to be there.

Oh daddy dear don't forget Dean,
He's got such a load to bear,
So daddy dear tell Jesus to help him,
To tarry on,
That at times when he thinks he can't stand up,
And spread the wonderful word,
That your spirit will be there to encourage him on.

Oh daddy dear please tell Jesus,
That Nancy dear needs your help,
To bring these little ones,
Up there to be with you.
Julianna, Jeremy and Christopher,
Will miss you daddy dear very much,
So please tell Jesus to be there,
When they come home to mama dear.

Oh daddy dear since you're now gone
Brother Darrel will need Jesus,
To help him bear the load of
Great responsibility, because he is the oldest,
For mama dear will need advice,
Since you have gone to heaven daddy dear

So please tell Jesus brother needs help.

Oh daddy dear we want to tell you
What a wonderful daddy you have been to us,
You know there were times as we went through our life,
That us poor children grew up and thought,
We were pretty smart at times,
We thought we knew a little more than you daddy dear,
And there were times when us poor children,
Were not so nice, but daddy dear,
You never quit loving us children dear.

Oh daddy dear oh how we long some wonderful day
To join you up there what a wonderful time,
We will have that day and also daddy dear,
You won't be alone up there for David Leon and
  Myron Lynn
Will welcome you home with joyful tears.

Oh daddy dear we have to go
And make what we can of this home here below,
Life will be rough for awhile
We want to tell you now that this world here below,
Has never before seen a more wonderful daddy dear.
So Good-bye Daddy Dear!

Family #46—Herman Joe & Cindy Stutzman

Herman Joe Stutzman was born September 20, 1972, to Herman N. and Dorothy (Petersheim) Stutzman. He married Cindy Miller on September 20, 1995. She was born August 8, 1976, to Raymond E. and Elsie (Hostetler) Miller. Both sets of parents are living in the Clarita settlement.

After the wedding Herman Joe and Cindy moved to the Mel Troyer place which his parents owned. They had a dairy there and milked cows for two years.

Children

Marietta Sue	July 4, 1996
Geneva Marie	January 1, 1998
Dorothy Elaine	June 8, 1999

Herman Joe and Cindy lived on the Troyer place and had a dairy until they moved to Charlotte, Michigan.

Laurie Ann   May 27, 2001

Herman Joes moved to Charlotte, Michigan on July 28, 1997, where he was ordained minister and later bishop. He is a son of #22, brother to #37, #42, and #50. Cindy is a daughter of #1, sister to #32, #40, #41, #43, and #45.

Family #47—Daniel & Cathryn Troyer

Daniel Troyer was born August 9, 1963, to Ben B. and Emma (Mast) Troyer. He married Cathryn Schrock on April 24, 1986. She was born August 6, 1964, to Leroy and Sarah Schrock of Jamesport, Missouri.

Daniel and Cathryn set up housekeeping in Jamesport and lived there for one year. They then moved to Stephenville, Texas and worked on a dairy for almost two years.

Daniel and Cathryn Troyer's house. The family dog guards the place.

They moved back to Jamesport, Missouri and lived there for seven years.

On January 21, 1997, Daniels moved to Coal County, Oklahoma and bought the farm, 110 acres with buildings, from Joe and Edna Petersheim when they moved to Charlotte. They also bought ninety acres from Thomas Rice and have a full-time dairy and busy schedule. They milk around fifty cows.

Children

James	November 14, 1987
Kenneth	June 17, 1991
Loretta Sue	April 5, 1993
Steven Joni	February 10, 1996
Christopher Allen	July 13, 1998
Lisa Marie	December 3, 1999
Sara Kaylene	May 13, 2001

Daniel Troyers are busy on the dairy. They are full-time farmers.

The Amish cemetery on the Hershberger farm.

Susan Ilene   May 13, 2001 - Stillborn
Benjamin Leroy September 23, 2003

Daniels have three scholars. The oldest son, James, is out of school and a big help at home on the dairy farm. He works out part-time helping Norman Miller now and then and sometimes Gus Martin at the Martin Hereford Ranch.

Daniel does some custom baling in the summer and does part-time carpenter work. He worked for John Henry Miller's crew at first.

Daniels had twin daughters several years ago with one being stillborn (Susan Ilene). She is the fourth to be buried in the Amish cemetery.

Family #48—John & Kathy Troyer

John Troyer was born October 24, 1973, to Ben B. and Emma (Mast) Troyer. He married Kathy Ann Hostetler on

John and Kathy Ann lived here before they built their store and home on Ben B. Troyers' farm.

October 17, 1996. She was born June 17, 1974, to Bill and Ada Hostetler of Jamesport, Missouri.

John and Kathy Ann lived in Jamesport, Missouri the first year after their marriage. They moved to Coal County, Oklahoma in the fall of 1997. They first moved and rented on the place where Perry Summys had lived. There is a house there now instead of a trailer.

Johns built a store building and a home all in one on Ben B. Troyers' field (his parents) and started a Bent and Dent store in 1998. They moved to the new building as soon as it was finished and had the store business until the first part of 2000, when they quit the store business and John took over John Henry Miller's construction crew. In November of 2002, John quit the construction crew and is working at home. They also raise Bernice Mountain dogs and Bull

Mastiffs.

Their land is used for parking space for the annual school auction.

Children

Paul Andrew	March 23, 1998
Emily Ann	November 13, 1999

Johns' store building and where they now live.

Rebecca Faye	March 28, 2001
Regina Marie	February 24, 2003
Matthew John	April 9, 2004

John and Kathy Ann are in the process of taking over his parents, Ben and Emma Troyers' 278-acre farm at the present time.

Family #49—David & Miriam Yoder

David H. Yoder was born August 22, 1953, to Henry and

Elsie (Bender) Yoder of Dover, Delaware. He married Miriam Wagler on July 6, 1978. She was born February 3, 1958, to Enos and Mary (Kuepfer) Wagler of Ontario, Canada.

Children

David Enos	November 30, 1979
Elsie Mae	December 18, 1980
Daniel Ray	December 22, 1981
John Henry	March 29, 1983
Melvin Jay	April 5, 1984
Elizabeth Ann	May 5, 1985
Levi Reuben	August 30, 1995

David and Miriam moved to Coal County, Oklahoma with their family on June 3, 1999, from Clyde, New York.

Davids had beef cattle to begin with. They bought the Mel Troyer place from Herman Stutzmans, so maybe we can

This is where David H. Yoders now live. You can see the steps that lead to the boys' rooms to the right lean at the shop.

The turkey guards the place at Davids, so expect him to meet you when you drive in.

now refer to this place as the David Yoder place.

David is now a mechanic, and has a shop where he repairs machinery and equipment. Their son John worked out on carpenter jobs the first two years but now helps at home in the shop too. The two girls teach school (Elsie, twenty-two years, Elizabeth, seventeen, is her helper) at Elm Creek School.

The boys' bedrooms are out by the shop where they added an addition upstairs on one side. The stairway goes up from the outside. This makes nice rooms for growing boys.

Visitors are greeted by seven-year-old Levi who is a very friendly boy. But the turkey gobbler that also likes to greet people is sometimes not as friendly. So if you pay a visit look for Levi, but beware of the turkey!

Nathan and Anna Stutzman's house. The bench wagon is there which indicates they just had church services.

Family #50—Nathan & Anna Stutzman

Nathan Lee Stutzman was born August 23, 1978, to Herman and Dorothy (Petersheim) Stutzman. He married Anna Mary Detweiler on October 12, 1999, at Charlotte, Michigan. She was born January 13, 1978, to Freeman and Emma (Gingerich) Detweiler.

Nathan and Anna moved to Coal County, Oklahoma after their wedding in Charlotte. The first year they lived in a trailer in back of Herman Stutzmans on the Davidson place that Hermans bought. This is on past the schoolhouse.

Nathan then bought an eighty-acre farm (across the railroad tracks to the west) from Jim Turner. This place is better known as the Leroy Magnes place.

Nathan worked on the carpenter crew for the first two years. They then decided to try goat farming. They have twenty-five dairy goats and quite a unique little goat setup. Their goats' milk goes to Atoka once a week to another goat dairy and from there they take it to Dallas, Texas. Here it is made into goats' cheese. During the summer they have to find another market for their milk.

Nathans have Alpine goats. Also Nubian, La Mancha, and Sanne. They have a Jersey cow which they milk to feed the baby goats with. They have a pail with six nipples with which they can feed six baby goats at one time. This is quite a sight and very interesting.

Children

Beth Ann	September 17, 2000
Marie Diane	August 20, 2001
David Wayne	November 14, 2002
Elmina Jo	April 23, 2004

Nathans have a goat dairy. This is the goat barn.

The little girls enjoy being out in the goat barn at milking time. Baby David Wayne watches from his car seat or sitter

Inside the goat barn. Nathan made his own unique setup.

Milking time for these goats. Four at a time with twenty-five nannies in all. Very interesting.

Anna feeds the baby goats while Nathan is milking. This pail feeds six little goats at one time.

Grain, hay, and water is put before the little ones, so they can eat at their leisure.

from on top of the bulk tank if he isn't sleeping, while his mother Anna helps husband Nathan in the goat barn or is outside feeding the baby goats in the goat pens.

Floyd J. Borntrager, born June 18, 1949, married April 23, 1970, to Lizzie D. Kauffman, born on November 23, 1950. They moved to Clarita on July 30, 2003.
Children

Floyd Jr.	March 26, 1971
Lucy	April 17, 1972
Daniel	May 3, 1973
Mary	September 8, 1974
Joseph	August 28, 1976
Ella Mae	February 24, 1978
Andrew	May 20, 1979
Ada	November 26, 1980
David	April 9, 1982
Emma	January 14, 1984

Andrew Borntrager, born May 20, 1979, married Verna Schrock on August 20, 2003. Verna was born on November 23, 1978. Andy moved to Clarita on March 10, 2003, and Verna moved here on August 26, 2003.

John Henry Yoder, born on March 29, 1983, married on October 15, 2003, to Rachel Ann Stutzman, born on June 13, 1982.

William Kauffman was born on September 30, 1982. He married Emma Borntrager on June 3, 2004. Emma was born on January 14, 1984.

Weddings that took place in the Clarita Settlement

Leroy (Elmers) Yoder & Lena (Dans) Mast
September 29, 1983

Allen (Nelsons) Yoder & Mary (Melvins) Hershberger
April 17, 1986

Edward (Elmers) Yoder & Ruby (Dans) Mast
April 30, 1987

Freeman (Emanuels) Yoder & Ada (Melvins) Hershberger
October 15, 1987

Edwin (Raymonds) Miller & Esther (Bens) Troyer
May 31, 1990

Andrew (Andys) Miller & Irene (Joes) Mast
December 3, 1992

Robert (West Union, Ohio) Raber & Susan (Raymonds) Miller
September 17, 1993

Paul (Milroy, Indiana) Kemp & Laura (Bens) Troyer
March 30, 1995

Reuben (Raymonds) Miller & Nancy (Harveys) Troyer
April 6, 1995

Herman Joe (Hermans) Stutzman & Cindy (Raymonds) Miller
September 20, 1995

Marlin (Dundee, Ohio) Beachy & Mary (Raymonds) Miller
May 7, 1999

John Henry (Davids) Yoder & Rachel Ann (Hermans) Stutzman
October 15, 2003

Toby (Roys) Miller & Miriam Sue (Hermans) Stutzman
December 30, 2004

Deaths in the Clarita Amish Settlement

Place of Burial

Polly P. Miller	March 13, 1985	Centerville, Michigan
Katie D. Troyer	July 17, 1985	Clarita, Oklahoma
Lena Mast	December 27, 1986	Kalona, Iowa
Rachel Sue Miller	February 24, 1990	Clarita, Oklahoma
Noah J. Coblentz	November 29, 1992	Hartville, Ohio
Elsie Marie Troyer	June 17, 1999	Clarita, Oklahoma
Susan Ilene Troyer	May 13, 2001	Clarita, Oklahoma
Anna Coblentz	January 23, 2002	Hartville, Ohio
Rachel Ann Yoder	October 29, 2004	Clarita, Oklahoma

There are five burials in the Clarita Amish Cemetery at Melvin Hershbergers' farm.

Katie D. Troyer was the first burial.

Born November 24, 1922—Died July 17, 1985

In memory of our dear mother and grandmother

K-atie, the name of our dear mother,
A-lways a smile and kind to others.
T-en years ago, it seems so long,
I-t was July of '85 that you joined the throng.
E-ternity, way beyond the blue.

D-ear Mother, how we miss you!

S-isters three, since have gone,
C-ame to join you ere long.
H-appy reunion in glory land,
L-ovely to hear the angel band.
A-lthough at times we shed tears,
B-eautiful memories we hold dear.
A-ngels guard us, guide us too.

C-hrist is coming soon, 'tis true.
H-eaven's door will open wide.

T-hen God will judge, meek or pride.
R-emember, let us all prepare,
O-thers we hope to meet up there.
Y-es, our deeds before us lain,
E-ternity in Heaven is our gain,
R-emembrance is a golden chain.
Written by Susan in 1995

"Mother"
We can only have one mother,
No one else can take her place.
How much she's needed, you'll never know,
Till you miss her loving face.
Be careful how you answer her,
And choose each word you say.
For remember she's your mother,
Though now she's old and gray.

Many tears you have caused her,
When you were bad or ill.
Many, many sleepless nights, though grown, you cause
her still.
So every time you leave her,
Matters not how far you go.
Part with a kind word and a smile,
You'll never regret it you know.

We can only have one mother,
Oh, take her to your heart.
You know not when the time will come,
That you and she must part.

Let her know you love her dearly,
Cheer and comfort her each day.
You can never have another,
When she has passed away.
-Author unknown

Second burial in Clarita Amish cemetery was Rachel Sue Miller, daughter and only child of Norman and Sylvia (Yoder) Miller, born December 30, 1981. Departed this world in the bloom of her life in a truck-buggy accident February 24, 1990 at the tender age of eight years, one month, and twenty-five days.

Norman and Sylvia sent in this poem:

A precious one from us is gone,
A voice we loved is stilled;
A place is vacant in our home,
Which never can be filled.

A sudden change so quickly fell,
Without a chance to say farewell;
Her willing hands and smiling face,
We see no more around the place.

To all of you who have a daughter,
Cherish her with good care;
You'll never know the heartache,
Till you find she isn't there.

When we think of you, dear Rachel,
How our eyes fill up with tears;
Life will be, oh, so lonely,
Since no words from you we hear.

Friends may think we have forgotten,
When at times they see us smile;

But little they know the heartaches,
That our smile hides all the while.
　　　　-The lonely parents

Another poem in memory of Rachel Sue in 1995

R-achel Sue, our only child you were,
A-nd born 1981, the 30th of December.
C-ome February 24, 1990, that morning,
H-e called from Heaven without warning.
E-nroute in horse and buggy to school,
L-oving memories remain of our jewel.

S-uddenly a semi hit from behind.
U-nconcious became your little mind.
E-MS and friends came to help so kind.

M-att. 6:33, the last words you said,
I-n the ditch your New Testament laid.
L-ittle we had known death was so near,
L-ife the next morn fled of our dear.
E-ternity with Jesus you now abide,
R-esting safely on the other side.
　　　Loved and Remembered,
　　　Norman & Sylvia

Third burial in Clarita Amish Cemetery was Elsie Marie Troyer, daughter of Levi and Lovina (Miller) Troyer, born October 1, 1996. Departed this world on June 17, 1999, in a farm accident.

In memory of Elsie Miller

Little Angels
When God calls little children to dwell with Him above,

We mortals sometimes question the wisdom of His love,
For no heartache compares with the death of a small child,
Who does so much to make our world seem so mild.

Perhaps God tires of calling the aged to His fold,
So He picked a rosebud before it can grow old.
God knows how much we need them, so He takes but a few,
To make the land of Heaven more beautiful to view.

Believing this is difficult, still somehow we must try,
The saddest word mankind knows is still "good-bye".
So when a little child departs, we who are left behind,
Must realize God loves children, angels are hard to find.

Sweet little Elsie, a namesake too,
Is happy in Heaven, far beyond the blue.
God called down from the angels' dome,
My dear little darling, arise and come.
To the place prepared in our Father's home.
She shall play with the angels on the golden streets;
She was much too fair and had grown too sweet
For the earth down here where we mortals meet.

Fourth burial in Clarita Amish cemetery
Stillborn twin daughter of Daniel and Cathryn Troyer

In Memory of Susan Ilene
  The Master Gardener from Heaven above,
  Planted two seeds in the Garden of Love.
  And from it there grew two rosebuds small,
  But one never had opportunity to open at all.

  Susan Ilene was the one God chose,
  To leave the earth for His Garden above.
  Where roses always bloom and never die,
  Though she never bloomed here, she will bloom on high.

So while you can't see your precious rose bloom,
You know the Great Gardener from the "Upper Room"
Is watching and tending this wee rose with care,
Tenderly touching each petal so fair.

So think of your darling with the angels above,
Secure and contented, surrounded by Love.
Remember God blessed and enriched your lives too,
Through this He brought Heaven closer to you.

Twin sister, Sara Kaylene, alone you'll trod,
To grow up with family, while I'm with God.
My dear, take courage, do not stray, no, never
So we can reunite someday, for ever and ever.

Fifth burial in Clarita Amish cemetery was Rachel Ann
Yoder, young wife of John Henry Yoder and young mother
to two month old Magdalena Ruth. She died of complica-
tions started by strep throat. It was very unexpected.

In Memory of Rachel Ann
A young wife so fair, a mother to a baby so small,
We trust God in heaven knows the meaning of it all.
Days are lonely, tears fall freely, hearts are heavy too,
So Jesus, walk with us daily, is our prayer to You.
Her life, a beautiful memory, her absence a silent grief,
Now she sleeps in God's beautiful garden in perfect peace.